Sauces

101 Handcrafted & Wholesome

Pirk • Billey • Paré • Darcy

Distributed by
Canada Book Distributors
www.canadabookdistributors.com
www.companyscoming.com
Tel: 1-800-661-9017

Library and Archives Canada Cataloguing in Publication

Title: Sauces: handcrafted & wholesome / Pirk, Billey, Paré, Darcy.
Other titles: Company's coming
Names: Pirk, Wendy, 1973- author. | Billey, Ashley, author. | Paré, Jean, 1927- author. Darcy, James, 1956- author.
Description: Includes index.
Identifiers: Canadiana 2021038204X | ISBN 9781772070491 (softcover)
Subjects: LCSH: Sauces. | LCGFT: Cookbooks.
Classification: LCC TX819.A1 B45 2022 | DDC 641.81/4,Äîdc23

Cover: *GettyImages:* Roxiller; VeselovaElena; travellinglight; WS Studio.

All inside photos by Company's coming except:
GettyImages: alexbai, 33; ALLEKO, 13, 99, 136; allhive, 131; AmalliaEka, 41, 150; AmalliaEka, 150; bhofack2, 27, 95, 127, 153; BWFolsom, 167; carlosrojas20, 157, 165; Caziopeia, 59; ChefPhotography, 57; Christophe Huchet, 18; Dar1930, 17, 31; dkgilbey, 75; DmitryLaptev, 14; DronG, 97; Eising, 67; evgenyb, 65; EzumeImages, 101; FatManPhotoUK, 89; format35, 51; freeskyline, 53; from_my_point_of_view, 139; geckophotos, 28; Giulia Verdinelli Photography, 49; gkrphoto, 60; grafvision, 83; grandriver, 137; HandmadePictures, 85, 123; iofoto, 23; istetiana, 187; JackF, 79; JanMacuch, 77; KPS, 148; joannatkaczuk, 39; Karaidel, 129; KarpenkovDenis, 20; La_vanda, 73, 87; LarisaBlinova, 135; LightFieldStudios, 191; los_angela, 113; Bartosz Luczak, 117, 145; mamypuk, 120; margouillatphotos, 37, 179; merc67, 181; MIND_AND_I, 173; Magone, 183; Manu_Bahuguna, 133; Marihakitchen, 119, 171; MarkSkalny, 109; Michelle Lee Photography, 21; Monkey Business Images, 14, 47; mpessaris, 177; Yusfa Hidayatul Murteza, 120; natalisla, 72; NSA Digital Archive, 90; OksanaKiian, 35, 147; OlgaLepeshkina, 161; Olha_Afanasieva, 43; Onradio, 25; opotishka, 175; piyato, 103; Igor Ploskin, 115; rafael_fernandes, 93; reamBigPhotos, 185; repinanatoly, 1, 190; Rimma_Bondarenko, 188; sebasnoo, 63; ShyMan, 45; smirart, 189; StephanieFrey, 169; StreetFlash, 154; svariophoto, 69, 81; tbralnina, 159; travellinglight, 125; ttsz, 72; vanillaechoes, 105, 107; vikif, 55, 71; vm2002, 163; Tatiana Volgutova, 15; WS Studio, 172; yasuhiroamano, 111, 112. *Wikimedia:* Auguste_Escoffier, 10; Cuisinierfrancois, 8; M-A-Careme, 9.

We acknowledge the financial support of the Government of Canada.
Nous reconnaissons l'appui financier du gouvernement du Canada.

Funded by the Government of Canada
Financé par le gouvernement du Canada | Canadä

Printed in China
PC: 38-1

The Company's Coming Story

Jean Paré, the founder of Company's Coming, grew up understanding that the combination of family, friends and home cooking is the best recipe for a good life.

"Never share a recipe you wouldn't use yourself."

Jean has mentored and inspired her team of chefs and cooks to embrace her ideals and approach to recipe creation based on tried-and-true testing.

Early in her career, Jean volunteered to prepare a dinner for more than 1,000 people attending the 50th anniversary celebration of the Vermillion School of Agriculture, now Lakeland College. From there, she launched a flourishing catering operation.

As requests for her recipes increased, Jean was often asked, "Why don't you write a cookbook?" The release of 150 Delicious Squares on April 14, 1981, marked the debut of what would soon turn into one of the world's most popular cookbook series, now with more than 350 titles.

Company's Coming cookbooks are distributed in Canada, the United States and other world markets. Bestsellers many times over in English, Company's Coming cookbooks have also been published in French and Spanish.

Familiar and trusted in home kitchens around the world, Company's Coming cookbooks are offered in a variety of formats. Highly regarded as kitchen workbooks, the softcover Original Series, with its lay-flat comb binding, is still a favourite among home cooks.

Jean Paré's approach to cooking has always called for quick and easy recipes using everyday ingredients. That view served her well, and the tradition continues in the Practical Gourmet series. The chefs in our test kitchens have been inspired by Jean's leadership and guidance to carry on her passion for sharing great recipes with home cooks.

Jean's Golden Rule of Cooking is: *Never share a recipe you wouldn't use yourself.* It's an approach that has worked—millions of times over!

Table of Contents

Introduction

Although we know very little of the food-preparation habits of our early ancestors, it is likely that as long as people have been preparing food, they have been experimenting with ways to make it taste good. Salt is one of the earliest seasonings that was important to ancient civilizations, both for flavour and for preservation. The archeological record indicates that people have been using locally available herbs for millennia, potentially for medicinal benefits as well as for flavour. When people began creating sauces to flavour food is unknown, but fish sauces were used to season food by the Zhou Dynasty (1046–256 BCE) in China, and an early form of soy sauce appeared during the Han Dynasty (206 BCE–220 CE). The ancient Greeks also used a fish sauce, called *garum*, that was adopted by the Roman Empire and featured heavily in their food until the fall of the empire. In Mesoamerica, the Maya and Aztecs seasoned their food with sauces made from crushed chili peppers.

A longstanding theory among food historians was that sauces were used to cover up the taste of food that was of dubious freshness thanks to the lack of refrigeration. While there may be some validity to this theory, it doesn't apply to sauces in much of Europe from the Roman Empire on through to Medieval times. Food preparation during this time was less about flavour and more about health. Specifically, food was used to balance one's "humors." A highly influential ancient Greek physician named Galen of Pergamum (130–260 CE), who worked for the Roman emperor Marcus Aurelius, devised a medical theory called humoral physiology. He believed the human body had four humors—blood, phlegm, yellow bile (choler) and black bile (melancholy.) To remain healthy, people needed to balance all four humors. Foods were ascribed different properties (dry, cold, hot, moist), and these properties aligned with the various humors. Blood was hot and moist; phlegm was cold and moist; yellow bile was hot and dry; and black bile was cold and dry. The foods you ate to maintain good health depended on what humor was out of balance in your system. So, for example, if you had too much phlegm (cold/moist) you would choose foods that were hot and dry to balance that particular humor. If your humors were in balance, you would choose food that balanced all four humors to keep them that way. Sauces were a great way to balance the humors in foods. This theory dominated food culture for hundreds of years and was adopted (and adapted) by civilizations after the Romans, including the Byzantine Empire, the Islamic empire and much of Europe until the Renaissance. At some point during the Middle Ages, cooks began adding sauces with flavour in mind to complement or contrast the dishes they were creating, but still following the humor principles. By the early Renaissance, these principles began to fall out of fashion as chefs became more interested in how food tasted and started breaking Galen's dietary guidelines to make their dishes more enjoyable. By the late Renaissance, meat drippings and butter were added to sauces, completely contradicting the humor dietetic view (Galen would have been aghast, had he been around to see it), and before long, humoral physiology was tossed aside, and the trend towards rich, flavourful sauces began.

Wealth was another factor that influenced the development of sauces in Europe (and most likely elsewhere, as well). Before the Age of Discovery, spices were extremely expensive in Europe. Because they were unaffordable for the masses, spices became a status symbol, and the rich showed off their wealth by incorporating as many exotic spices as possible into their dishes, even if the flavours were not complementary. Once Europeans sailors had direct access to the Spice Islands and other spice sources in the East, the price of spices dropped, and they became more affordable for all levels of society. The elite needed another way to distinguish themselves from the masses, and so they incorporated ingredients such as milk and butter (again, too expensive for the masses) into their sauces. The French, in particular, eventually gained near-global recognition for the quality and richness of their sauces.

WHAT EXACTLY IS A SAUCE?

There is much debate about what exactly constitutes a sauce. Is ketchup a sauce or a condiment? For that matter, can a condiment be considered a sauce? Perhaps the best way to answer this question is to consider the purpose of a sauce. If it is simply to cover a dish or make a dish taste better, then there is a lot of room for interpretation. If that is the case, then condiments can indeed be sauces, as can such things as gremolata, which one might not traditionally think of as a sauce.

For this book, a sauce must meet the following criteria to be considered a sauce. It must be a compound not simply one ingredient. It must be put on a meal to make it taste better but be distinct from the actual dish, not simply an ingredient in the dish (for example, vinegar would be an ingredient in a dish, not a sauce.) The sauce cannot stand alone, but the dish it is added to can be eaten without it. With these criteria, some condiments can indeed be considered sauces.

In fact, condiment sauces hold a unique position because they allow individuals to personalize a dish to their liking, rather than having the flavour of their meal determined by the cook. Also noteworthy is that condiment sauces tend to keep more of their regional/national character because they were more often used by common folk out of what was locally available rather than by the upper classes, who could afford to incorporate more expensive and imported ingredients.

There are many packaged sauces available on the market today, but nothing you can buy at the supermarket can ever beat homemade. The best sauces need the best ingredients to really shine, and packaged sauces tend to contain preservatives, thickeners or other questionable ingredients. As the French could tell you, sauces are an artform that deserve the freshest ingredients and the time and care necessary to coax the ingredients together into a liaison that will thrill the palate and transform your meal from basic food to an amazing meal.

French Cuisine: A Historical Perspective

In fine dining circles, French cuisine is respected as *haute cuisine*, the best there is, and this is largely due to the sauces. French cuisine is such a big part of fine dining that the terminology for cooking techniques and the names of the sauces are French words, even in English-speaking countries (for example, Hollandaise Sauce is not Dutch sauce in English).

To be clear, when it emerged, modern French cuisine was not the cuisine of France. It was the cuisine of the upper classes throughout much of Europe, far out of reach of most of the population. This style of cooking arose during the reign of Louis XIV. By the mid-17th century, France was a major cultural centre. Under the reign of Louis XIV, also known as Louis the Great, France was a dominant political power and a leader in the arts and sciences. The extravagant Palace of Versailles was being transformed into the most grandiose palace in all of Europe, boasting beautiful gardens, paintings and other artwork. It wasn't just a place for the king to live; it was basically its own city, housing the French government, nobility and army as well as hundreds of servants, gardeners and chefs. To meet Louis' exacting standards, chefs had to prepare lavish meals, with food that was rich and decadent with an elegant presentation. In fact, the look of the food was just as important as the way it tasted. This was the beginning of *haute cuisine*.

L E

CUISINIER

FRANÇOIS,

o v

EST ENSEIGNE' LA MANIERE
d'apprêter toute forte de viandes,
de faire toute forte de Patifferies,
& de Confitures.

Reveu, & augmenté d'un Traité de Confitures
féiches & liquides, & pour apprêter des feftins
aux quatre Saifons de l'Année.

Par le Sieur DE LA VARENNE
Ecuyer de Cuifine de Monfieur
le Marquis d'Vxelles.

UNZIE'ME EDITION,

A LYON,

Chez JACQUES CANIER, rüe
Confort, au Chef S. Jean.

M. DC. LXXX.
AVEC PERMISSION,

One of the most important and influential chefs of this time was François-Pierre de la Varenne (1618–78). His cookbook, *La Cuisinier Francois*, published 1651, was the first French cookbook to be translated into English (in 1653) and stayed in print for more than a century. La Varenne can be seen as a transitional figure between Medieval cookery and modern *haute cuisine*. Although many of his recipes had Medieval elements, he broke from the Medieval rules of cooking and humoral physiology, and focused on flavour instead. Many of his ideas influenced how French cuisine grew into the highly respected phenomenon it is today. He promoted the idea that flavours in food should complement each other, instead of contrasting, as was the Medieval mindset. As such, he made sauces with an extract of the dish they were serving (e.g., poultry dishes were served with poultry-based sauces), so the flavours in the dish were harmonious. He is also credited with inventing the roux for thickening sauces instead of breadcrumbs. Perhaps most importantly, however, was the culinary logic of his recipes. From his work came the idea that a few basic stocks could be kept on hand and reduced to form the fountation for a variety of other sauces. This idea was expanded upon more than 150 years later by the "Father of Sauces" Marie-Antonin Carême.

Carême (1784–1833) was perhaps the most influential chef in France's history and has been credited with developing *haute cuisine* as we know it today. He is best known for his classification system of French sauces, establishing a hierarchy in which a "mother sauce" forms the base for many secondary or "daughter" sauces, which can then be used to make even more sauces (which we could call "granddaughter sauces," although he did not). Mother sauces were meant to be foundation sauces—the building blocks for a variety of sauces—not generally used on their own. He named Allemande, Bechamel, Espagnole and Velouté as mother sauces and then organized the sauces that could be derived from each of them. Once the mother sauce system was in place, new sauces were added rapidly, and these were named after historic

Marie-Antoine Carême

people or events. Some of the histories for the sauces can be confirmed, but even the ones that can't be reveal a lot about the history of the period. At this point in history, sauces became so important that a bad cook was called a *gâte-sauce*, "sauce spoiler."

Carême also built a structure for preparing the sauces that was clear and adaptable; the sauces themselves might be complicated, but the method is clear. First, start with a reduced stock, add the "liason" to make the mother sauce, then add the seasonings and other flavouring to make the secondary sauce and so on. La Varenne introduced a simple version of the structure in his cookbook—building a sauce out of a reduced stock—but Carême adapted and expanded it, carefully documenting the steps so they could be recreated. He systemized other aspects of cuisine in the same way, organizing steps that built off the previous step to create a complete dish. French *haute cuisine* in Carême's day was daunting, with complicated, fussy techniques that had to be learned through apprenticeships. Carême wrote several cookbooks that described in great detail how various recipes should be prepared. He is probably best known for his encyclopedic 5-volume *L'art de la Cuisine Française au XIXe siècle*, published in 1832. His system stood until the late 1800s, when a French chef named August Escoffier entered the culinary scene.

Escoffier (1846–1935), called "the King of Chefs and the Chef of Kings" by Germany's Kaiser Wilhelm II, is best known for simplifying and modernizing *haute cuisine*. He adapted Carême's sauce classification system, adding Tomato Sauce and Hollandaise as mother sauces, and demoting Allemande to a daughter sauce of Velouté. He also championed the use of seasonal ingredients and eschewed the elaborate garnishes that had been so popular in Carême's day.

Auguste Escoffier

Escoffier also streamlined the *haute cuisine* kitchen, implementing *la brigade de cuisine*, based on a military chain of command that he witnessed while serving as an army chef during the Franco-Prussian war. In this system, which is still used today in commercial kitchens, every cook has a specific role or station, so the kitchen can function efficiently. Although Escoffier originally assigned more than 20 roles in the brigade, today there are only five that remain. The *Chef Executif* (executive chef) isn't part of the kitchen staff and is responsible for more business-oriented tasks, such as managing the restaurant (or a chain of restaurants) and marketing. The *Chef de Cuisine* (head chef) is responsible for the day-to-day running of the kitchen and menu-planning, and answers to the executive chef or restaurant owner. The *Sous-chef de Cuisine* (sous-chef) is the second in command in the kitchen. They oversee each station in the kitchen and answer to the head chef. A *Chef de Partie* is responsible for a particular station in the kitchen, which could include a *Saucier* (sauce chef); *Grillardin* (grill chef), *Entremetier* (entree chef) and *Patissier* (pastry chef), to name a few. A *Commis Chef* is basically a floater, helping out wherever needed, so they must know all the stations in the kitchen.

Escoffier also changed how food was served to restaurant patrons. Before Escoffier, *haute cuisine* used the *table d'hôte* system, in which a diner could only order a set multi-course meal, and all the courses were served at the same time. Escoffier changed the *table d'hote* system to allow each course to be served separately in a specific order. He also instituted the *à la carte* system, which gave diners the freedom to choose individual dishes they preferred instead of being limited to ordering the full multi-course meal.

French cuisine is constantly evolving as new ingredients and techniques are introduced, but it is safe to say that without the work of la Varenne, Carême and Escoffier, French cuisine would not enjoy the respect and esteem that is does today.

Béchamel

Mornay	Cheddar Cheese	Soubise	Moutade / Mustard	Nantua	Crème / Cream

Espagnole / Brown

Bordelaise	Madère / Madeira	Chasseur / Hunter	Bercy	Estragon / Tarragon	Diable	Duxelles

Tomate / Tomato

Portugaise / Portuguese	Espagnole Tomate / Spanish	Creole

Velouté

Veloute-Fish Stock	Veloute-Chicken Stock	Veloute-Veal Stock
Bercy	Hongroise / Hungarian	Bonnefoy
Estragon / Tarragon	Aurore / Aurora	Horseradish
Normande / Normandy	Currie / Curry	Villageoise
Vin Blanc / White Wine Crevettes / Shrimp, Chivry / Herb, Vénitienne / Venetian	Suprême / Supreme Champignon / Mushroom, Ivoire / Ivory, Albufera	Allemande Poulette, Estragon / Tarragon

Classic Hollandaise

Maltaise	Mousseline	Divine	Classic Béarnaise Creamy Béarnaise	Choron

Mayonnaise

Aioli	Remoulade	Tartar

Béchamel

Perhaps the best known and easiest of the mother sauces, Béchamel is a rich, creamy white sauce that can be served as is or used as a base for more complex sauces. This sauce's origin is unclear. One theory suggests that it is French in origin and was created by the chef of Louis de Béchamel, an aristocrat who lived during the time of Louis XIV. Another theory suggests that the sauce dates back to 16th century Italy and was brought to France by the cooks of Catherine de' Medici when she married Henry II in 1533. LaVarenne, author of the influential 1651 cookbook *Le Cuisinier François*, is often credited with publishing the first recipe for Béchamel Sauce as it is known today. Whereas early versions of the sauce were bound with egg, his version, like today's Béchamel, was bound with a roux.

Whole cloves	6	6
Bay leaf	1	1
Medium onion	1/4	1/4
Milk	4 cups	1 L
Butter	6 tbsp.	90 mL
All-purpose flour	6 tbsp.	90 mL
White pepper	1 tsp.	5 mL
Salt	1 tsp.	5 mL
Nutmeg	1/2 tsp.	2 mL

To make an onion piqué (see page 13), use cloves to pin bay leaf to onion, pushing cloves through leaf and into onion like thumb tacks. Press any remaining cloves into onion.

Heat milk and onion piqué in a heavy saucepan on medium until small bubbles begin to form along edge of pot, just before it reaches a simmer. Keep milk at this stage for about 10 minutes, stirring occasionally.

Melt butter in a medium saucepan on low heat. Whisk in flour to form a roux. Cook, whisking constantly, for about 1 minute.

Remove onion piqué from milk and discard. Slowly add hot milk to roux, whisking constantly to prevent lumps. Bring mixture to a boil and then reduce heat to a simmer. Whisk in white pepper, salt and nutmeg. Cook, stirring occasionally, for about 10 minutes. Remove from heat and serve. If sauce is not being used immediately, set aside to cool. Once it is cool, place a sheet of wax paper or pour a thin layer of milk or melted butter over top to prevent a skin from forming and store in an airtight container in refrigerator for up to 3 days. Makes 4 cups (1 L).

An onion piqué is a French culinary technique that allows you to add flavour to a sauce without adding chunks or colour. In the traditional onion piqué, cloves are pushed through bay leaves into the flesh of a raw onion. As the sauce cooks, the onion, bay leaves and cloves release their flavour but can be easily removed from the sauce before it is served, leaving it silky smooth.

Mornay

Mornay Sauce is Béchamel Sauce to which grated cheese has been added. Gruyere is the traditional cheese of choice, but other white cheeses, such as Parmesan, Swiss or white Cheddar are also sometimes used. Classic Mornay Sauce was enriched with egg yolks, but many chefs today choose to leave them out. Although Béchamel sauces enriched with cheese have been around much longer, classic Mornay Sauce is thought to date back to the late 19th century and has been attributed to Joseph Voiron, the chef of a prestigious Parisienne restaurant named Durand, who is said to have named it after his son. It is often served with chicken, eggs, fish, shellfish, vegetables and pasta.

Béchamel Sauce (see page 12)	**4 cups**	**1 L**
Grated Gruyere cheese	**1 cup**	**250 mL**
Grated Parmesan cheese	**1/4 cup**	**60 mL**

Keep Béchamel Sauce warm on low heat. Remove from heat and whisk in both cheeses. If sauce is too thick, whisk in a few spoonfuls of hot milk until it reaches your desired consistency. Sauce is best served immediately but can be stored in an airtight container in refrigerator for up to 3 days. Makes 5 cups (1.25 mL).

Cheddar Cheese

Although Cheddar Cheese Sauce seems to have originated in England, we've included it in with the French sauces because it uses Béchamel Sauce as its base. Cheddar Cheese Sauce can be thought of as England's version of Mornay Sauce, using their native Cheddar cheese in place of the traditional Gruyere. It is the classic sauce to use when making macaroni and cheese but pairs well with any pasta and is also tasty served over vegetables dishes.

Béchamel Sauce (see page 12)	4 cups	1 L
Grated Cheddar cheese	2 cups	500 mL
Worcestershire sauce	1/4 tsp.	1 mL
Dry mustard	1 tbsp.	15 mL

Remove warm Béchamel Sauce from heat and whisk in Cheddar cheese, Worcestershire sauce and dry mustard. Sauce is best served immediately but can be stored in an airtight container in refrigerator for up to 3 days. Makes about 5 1/2 cups (1.4 L).

Soubise

Soubise Sauce is Béchamel Sauce that has been enriched with cooked, pureed onions. The key to this sauce is to cook the onions without allowing them to brown. The onions are then blended into the sauce to make a smooth, rich and creamy sauce that is served with vegetables, poultry and eggs. It also makes an excellent base for casseroles. This sauce is thought to have been named in honour of Charles de Rohan, who was the Prince of Soubise in the mid-18th century and a marshal of France. It seems that his personal chef was the one who created this sauce, but at the time a mere chef did not warrant any recognition, so the sauce was credited to Charles de Rohan instead. Classic Soubise Sauce was thickened with pureed rice, but modern cooks usually leave the rice out.

Béchamel Sauce (see page 12)	**4 cups**	**1 L**
Butter	1/4 cup	60 mL
Thinly sliced onion	3 1/2 cups	875 mL

Keep Béchamel Sauce warm on medium-low heat.

Melt butter in a large frying pan on medium-low heat. Add onions and cook, stirring occasionally, until onions are soft, about 30 minutes. Do not let onions brown. Stir into Béchamel Sauce and cook on low heat for about 30 minutes to combine flavours, stirring occasionally so as not to burn bottom of sauce. Use an immersion blender to puree onions into sauce until smooth. Strain sauce through a fine-mesh sieve or a sieve lined with cheesecloth, discarding solids. Sauce is best served immediately but can be stored in an airtight container in refrigerator for up to 3 days. Makes about 6 1/2 cups (1.6 L).

Moutarde/Mustard

Mustard seed has a long history of use, first medicinally and then to flavour food. Although the ancient Sumerians, Egyptians and Greeks are known to have used mustard seed, the ancient Romans are credited with making the first mustard that resembles the condiment we know today. As the Roman Empire grew, and the Roman people spread out through the empire, mustard was introduced to much of the European continent. It is recorded in texts in France as early as the 1200s, and France was recognized as a main producer by the 1300s. It is not clear who first decided to add mustard to Béchamel Sauce, but the result was this delicious sauce that is excellent with pork, ham, eggs and poultry. You can change up the texture of the sauce by using a grainy Dijon, or use yellow mustard or a darker German coloured mustard to change the colour.

Béchamel Sauce (see page 12)	**2 cups**	**500 mL**
Prepared mustard	**1/4 cup**	**60 mL**

Remove warm Béchamel Sauce from heat and whisk in mustard. Sauce is best served immediately but can be stored in an airtight container in refrigerator for up to 3 days. Makes 2 1/4 cups (550 mL).

Nantua

Traditionally made with crayfish, Nantua Sauce was named after a town in eastern France that has long been respected for its cuisine and is renowned for its freshwater fish and crayfish. We've replaced the crayfish with shrimp in this recipe because shrimp is generally more readily available and affordable. Nantua Sauce is usually served with fish or seafood dishes, and is an integral part of Quenelles Nantua, fish dumplings in Nantua Sauce.

Butter, softened	6 tbsp.	90 mL
Parsley, finely chopped	1 tbsp.	15 mL
Lemon juice	1 tsp.	5 mL
White pepper	1/8 tsp.	0.5 mL
Cooked shrimp, finely chopped	1/4 cup	60 mL
Béchamel Sauce (see page 12)	**2 cups**	**500 mL**
Whipping cream	1/4 cup	60 mL

Combine first 5 ingredients in a small bowl, mixing well. Transfer mixture to a sheet of parchment or wax paper and roll into a cylinder, about 1 inch (2.5 cm) thick. Chill in refrigerator until firm.

Keep Béchamel Sauce warm on medium-low heat. Cut shrimp butter into pieces and whisk into sauce, 1 piece at a time, until all butter is incorporated. Slowly stir in cream. Sauce is best served immediately but can be stored in an airtight container in refrigerator for up to 3 days. Makes 2 1/2 cups (625 mL).

Crème/Cream

This classic cream sauce adds elegance to any meal. It is essentially a richer, creamier version of Béchamel. The lemon juice adds a bright, fresh touch. This sauce is excellent served over vegetables, eggs, poultry or poached fish. You can add a sprinkling of freshly chopped herbs at the end of the cooking time for a little splash of colour and visual interest.

Béchamel Sauce (see page 12)	**4 cups**	**1 L**
Whipping cream	**1 1/4 cups**	**300 mL**
Lemon juice	**2 tsp.**	**10 mL**

Keep Béchamel Sauce warm on medium-low heat.

Scald cream in a small pot on low heat (see below). Whisk into Béchamel Sauce.

Whisk in lemon juice. Sauce is best served immediately but can be stored in an airtight container in refrigerator for up to 3 days. Makes about 5 1/4 cups (1.3 L).

〰️ To scald cream, warm it in a double boiler over low heat, stirring constantly, until small bubbles appear along the sides of the pot. Do not overheat or the cream will be scorched instead of scalded.

Thickening Sauces

Despite your best efforts, sometimes your sauce does not turn out as thick and creamy as you were expecting it to. Thankfully, there are a number of ways you can salvage your sauce and turn it into the rich, creamy pièce de résistance it was meant to be. Three of the most common methods include reduction, adding a roux and adding a cornstarch slurry.

Reduction

Many of the classic French sauces use this technique to achieve the correct texture. To reduce a sauce, allow it to simmer, uncovered, on medium-low heat. As it simmers, some of the liquid will evaporate, thickening the sauce and condensing the flavours. This method can be quite time consuming, but if you have the time, the results are well worth the wait.

Using a Roux

A roux is another thickening agent that is used often in classic French sauces. In fact, three of the five Mother Sauces are thickened with a roux. A roux is a mixture of liquid fat (usually melted butter) and flour. Flour is a great thickener, but if you add it directly to your sauce, it will clump together instead of giving your sauce a thick, uniform texture. To prevent clumping, flour is mixed with melted butter so each individual starch granule in the flour gets coated with fat, which prevents them from sticking together. The mixture is whisked constantly as it cooks until it reaches the desired colour. There are four types of roux—white, blond, brown and dark brown—determined by the length of cooking time. A roux's ability to thicken decreases the longer it is cooked, so each type of roux has its own applications. French sauces use only the first three roux.

White: has the shortest cooking time and has a neutral flavour. It is the best thickener and is used in Béchamel.

Blond: has a longer cooking time, which gives it a slightly darker colour and a nutty aroma. It has less thickening ability than the white roux and is used for Velouté sauces.

Brown: is even darker than a blond roux, rather like the colour of peanut butter, with a stronger nutty flavour. It has even less thickening power than the two lighter roux and is used in Sauce Tomate (the mother Tomato Sauce) and Espagnole.

Dark Brown: is the longest cooked, darkest and most flavourful roux but has the least amount of thickening power. This roux is not used in the recipes in this book but is common in Cajun or Creole cooking, particularly in gumbos.

Cornstarch Slurry

A cornstarch slurry is a much quicker way to thicken a sauce. Unlike a roux, which has to be cooked before it can be added, a cornstarch slurry is added at the end of the cooking time. To use, simply mix cornstarch into cold water until smooth, then add to the hot sauce. This method is not generally used with French sauces, but it is well suited to many of the Asian sauces.

Espagnole/Brown

Another of the five mother sauces, Espagnole is the classic brown sauce, made by simmering brown stock with tomato puree, a *mirepoix* (see page 40) and sometimes fresh herbs, and thickened with a brown roux (see page 21). Prepared with the classic technique, it is the most time consuming and labour intensive of all the mother sauces, requiring plenty of skimming, stirring and straining. Most cooks today prepare a simplified version of this sauce, which is still rich and delicious. Espagnole Sauce is generally not served as is; it is primarily used as a foundation for other sauces. In classical French cuisine, it was mixed with an equal amount of brown stock and cooked until the mixture was reduced by half to make Demi-glace, which featured prominently in many French sauces.

As with many of the classic French sauces, the origin of this sauce is murky. One of the more popular theories suggests that it was named after the spicy sauces brought to France by Spanish cooks working for Maria Theresa, Infanta of Spain, when she married King Louis XIV in 1660. For a period in history, the sauce's foreign origins and name offended French nationalists, who thought it was an affront to French pride. Carême soothed their ruffled feathers, though, by highlighting the fact that the sauce honoured the past French queen, and by claiming that the sauce was elevated and perfected by French chefs and techniques.

Bay leaf	1	1
Dried thyme	1/2 tsp.	2 mL
Peppercorns	6	6
Parsley sprigs	2	2
Butter	1/2 cup	125 mL
Diced onion	3/4 cup	175 mL
Diced carrot	2/3 cup	150 mL
Diced celery	1/2 cup	125 mL
All-purpose flour	1/2 cup	125 mL
Brown stock (see page 23)	5 cups	1.25 L
Tomato puree (see page 55)	1/4 cup	60 mL
Salt	1 tsp.	5 mL
Pepper	1 tsp.	5 mL

Combine first 4 ingredients in a small piece of cheesecloth and tie with a piece of cooking twine to form a *bouquet garni*. Set aside.

Melt butter in a medium saucepan on medium. Add vegetables and cook, stirring occasionally, until onion is well caramelized, about 10 to 15 minutes.

Add flour and cook, stirring constantly, to make a brown roux (see page 21).

Gradually add stock and tomato puree, whisking constantly to break up any lumps of roux. Bring to a boil, then reduce heat to a simmer.

Add *bouquet garni,* salt and pepper, and simmer for 45 to 60 minutes, allowing sauce to reduce by a quarter. Skim surface as needed. Strain sauce through a fine-mesh sieve or a sieve lined with several layers of cheesecloth, discarding solids. Store in an airtight container in refrigerator for up to 7 days. Makes about 4 cups (1 L).

A brown stock is made by simmering browned beef or veal bones with aromatic vegetables, such as carrots, onion and celery, and fresh herbs. For a white stock, you would simmer raw (i.e., not browned) poultry (usually chicken) or veal bones with the same aromatic vegetables.

Bordelaise

This classic sauce is named after the famous vineyards of Bordeaux, which have existed since the Romans colonized the area around 50 CE. Although this sauce was originally made with white wine, since the early 20th century red wine has become the norm. The main differences between Bordelaise Sauce and its Espagnole base are the addition of red wine, and that Bordelaise Sauce is finished with butter and bone marrow. This sauce is traditionally served over filet mignon or with grilled beef or steak.

Espagnole Sauce (see page 22)	2 cups	500 mL
Red wine	1/2 cup	125 mL
Thinly sliced shallots	1/2 cup	125 mL
Bay leaf	1	1
Peppercorns, crushed	1/2 tsp.	2 mL
Ground thyme	1/4 tsp.	1 mL
Butter	2 tbsp.	30 mL
Bone marrow	1/2 cup	125 mL

Keep Espagnole Sauce warm on medium-low heat.

Heat next 5 ingredients in a small saucepan on medium. Cook, stirring often, until reduced by half. Add to Espagnole Sauce and cook, stirring occasionally, for 15 to 20 minutes. Strain sauce through a fine-mesh sieve or a sieve lined with cheesecloth. Discard solids and return sauce to saucepan.

Add butter and bone marrow, stirring constantly until melted. Sauce is best served immediately but can be stored in an airtight container in refrigerator for up to 5 days. Makes about 2 cups (500 mL).

Madère/Madeira

This simple brown sauce is enriched with Madeira, a fortified wine that is named for its place of origin, a Portuguese island off the coast of Morocco. The Madeira wine makes this rich sauce slightly sweet, perfect for serving with red meat, especially roasts and venison.

Espagnole Sauce (see page 22)	2 cups	500 mL
Madeira wine	1/4 cup	60 mL

Bring Espagnole Sauce and Madeira to a simmer in a medium saucepan on medium. Cook, stirring occasionally, until sauce has been reduced to 2 cups (500 mL). Sauce is best served immediately but can be stored in an airtight container in refrigerator for up to 5 days. Makes 2 cups (500 mL).

Bordelaise

Chasseur/Hunter

Chasseur Sauce has an Espagnole base to which white wine, mushrooms and tomatoes are added. Whereas most French sauces are silky smooth, this sauce is meant to be chunky, perhaps reflecting its "wild" or less refined roots. *Chasseur* is the French word for "hunter," and this sauce would traditionally have included wild mushrooms and been served over wild game, including venison, rabbit and birds such as pheasant—basically whatever the hunter was able to bag. Today this sauce is often served with steak, veal, pork and poultry.

Espagnole Sauce (see page 22)	**4 cups**	**1 L**
Butter	3 tbsp.	45 mL
Thinly sliced mushrooms	1 1/2 cups	375 mL
Thinly sliced shallots	1/3 cup	75 mL
White wine	1 1/2 cup	375 mL
Diced, seeded tomatoes	1 1/2 cups	375 mL
Chopped parsley	2 tbsp.	30 mL

Keep Espagnole Sauce warm on medium-low heat.

Melt butter in a medium saucepan on medium-low heat. Add mushrooms and shallots and cook, stirring often, until mushrooms are soft and shallots are translucent, about 6 minutes.

Increase heat to medium and add wine. Bring to a boil, and then reduce heat to a simmer. Cook until liquid is reduced to a quarter.

Whisk in Espagnole Sauce and tomatoes. Bring to a simmer and cook, stirring often, for about 10 minutes until sauce is thick enough to coat back of a spoon. Remove from heat and stir in parsley. Sauce is best served immediately but can be stored in an airtight container in refrigerator for up to 4 days. Makes about 5 cups (1.25 L).

Bercy

White wine and shallots transform the classic Espagnole into the savoury Bercy Sauce, which is generally served with roast beef or steak. This sauce gets its name from Bercy in Paris, which was originally a village outside of Paris but is now a district within the city. Bercy has long been associated with wine, and it became the centre of the French wine market in the 19th century. Situated on the banks of the Seine River, Bercy was perfectly placed to receive wines from Burgundy and ship them around the world. The area became known for its cheap wine and lively atmosphere, and it drew merchants, artisans and revelers from far and wide.

Espagnole Sauce (see page 22)	**2 cups**	**500 mL**
White wine	1 cup	250 mL
Thinly sliced shallots	3/4 cup	175 mL

Keep Espagnole Sauce warm on medium-low heat.

Heat wine and shallots in a medium saucepan on medium. Cook until reduced to about 1/4 cup (60 mL). Whisk in Espagnole Sauce and bring to a simmer. Cook, stirring often, for about 10 minutes until sauce is thick enough to coat back of a spoon. Sauce is best served immediately but can be stored in an airtight container in refrigerator for up to 5 days. Makes 2 cups (500 mL).

Estragon/Tarragon

This sauce also contains white wine but is flavoured with tarragon instead of the shallots found in Bercy Sauce. *Estragon* is the French word for "tarragon." This sauce works especially well with chicken but is also served with turkey, pork and veal.

Espagnole Sauce (see page 22)	**2 cups**	**500 mL**
White wine	1 1/2 cups	375 mL
Chopped tarragon	1/2 cup	125 mL
Chopped tarragon	3 tbsp.	45 mL

Keep Espagnole Sauce warm on medium-low heat.

Bring wine to a boil in a medium saucepan on medium heat. Reduce heat to a simmer and cook for about 10 minutes until wine is reduced by half. Stir in first amount of tarragon. Cover and turn off heat. Let mixture stand for about 20 minutes so tarragon can infuse wine. Remove cover and turn heat to medium-low. Whisk in Espagnole Sauce. Cook, stirring occasionally, for about 10 minutes, until sauce is reduced by a third. Strain sauce through a fine-mesh sieve or a sieve lined with several layers of cheesecloth, discarding solids.

Stir in second amount of tarragon. Sauce is best served immediately but can be stored in an airtight container in refrigerator for up to 5 days. Makes about 1 1/2 cups (375 mL).

Diable

Diable is the French word for devil, and as you would expect from its name, Diable Sauce is meant to be "fiery" or spicy, at least by French cuisine's standards. This sauce is often served with broiled chicken or roasted or braised pork. Traditionally it was served with poultry prepared *a la Diable*, in which the bird was spread with mustard, sprinkled with bread crumbs and broiled until golden brown.

Espagnole Sauce (see page 22)	**2 cups**	**500 mL**
White wine	1 cup	250 mL
White wine vinegar	1/2 cup	125 mL
Finely chopped shallots	1/4 cup	60 mL
Pepper	1 tsp.	5 mL
Ground cayenne pepper	1/2 tsp.	2 mL
Salt	1/4 tsp.	1 mL

Keep Espagnole Sauce warm on medium-low heat.

Combine next 6 ingredients in a medium saucepan on medium. Bring to a boil then reduce heat to a simmer. Cook until wine is reduced by about half. Whisk in Espagnole Sauce and cook, stirring often, for another 10 minutes until sauce is thick enough to coat back of a spoon. Sauce is best served immediately but can be stored in an airtight container in refrigerator for up to 5 days. Makes 2 1/2 cups (625 mL).

Duxelles

This sauce has an Espagnole base that is enriched with the classic French mushroom and shallot preparation known as duxelles. In this preparation, finely chopped mushrooms and shallots are cooked in butter until all moisture has evaporated, leaving behind an almost paste-like consistency. François Pierre de la Varenne, who was the chef of the Marquis d'Uxelles, has been credited with the creation of duxelles. La Varenne is the author of one of the earliest and most influential cookbooks on French cuisine, *Le Cuisinier François,* published in 1651. He did not call his mixture "duxelle," but it was named in his honour by future chefs who adopted the preparation.

Espagnole Sauce (see page 22)	**1 1/2 cups**	**375 mL**
Butter	3 tbsp.	45 mL
Finely chopped mushrooms (see Tip, below)	3 cups	750 mL
Finely chopped shallots	2 tbsp.	30 mL
Salt	1 tsp.	5 mL
Pepper	1/2 tsp.	2 mL
White wine	1/2 cup	125 mL
Tomato puree (see page 55)	1/4 cup	60 mL
Finely chopped parsley	2 tbsp.	30 mL

Keep Espagnole Sauce warm on medium-low heat.

Melt butter in a medium saucepan on medium-low heat. Add mushrooms and shallots. Cook, stirring occasionally, until mushrooms have released their liquid and it has evaporated. Stir in salt and pepper.

Turn heat to medium and add wine. Cook, stirring, until wine is reduced to about 3 tbsp. (45 mL).

Whisk in Espagnole Sauce and tomato puree. Simmer for 7 to 8 minutes to allow flavours to blend. Stir in parsley. Sauce is best served immediately but can be stored in an airtight container in refrigerator for up to 5 days. Makes about 2 cups (500 mL).

Tip: Any type of mushroom can be used to make duxelles, but it is best when a few wild mushrooms are included in the mix.

Duxelles is a main component of Beef Wellington and is also used to flavour soups and sauces, as a filling for pasta, in omelets or as a spread for toast or crostini. Duxelles Sauce is delicious served with grilled beef, eggs, pasta and potatoes.

Tomate/Tomato

This sauce is another of the five mother sauces in French cooking, and it is similar to but slightly different from your typical tomato pasta sauce. It forms the basis for several other *haute-cuisine* sauces, including Portugaise, Spanish and Creole. Although it is meant to be a base to build other recipes from, it can also be used as is and works well on grilled chicken or fish, as well as over pasta. This sauce was traditionally made with fresh tomatoes, rendered salt pork and veal broth, and was thickened with a roux. It is the roux that really separates the French Tomato Sauce from Italian versions, but some modern variations skip the roux and thicken the sauce by reduction instead.

Diced bacon	1/3 cup	75 mL
Butter	6 tbsp.	90 mL
Chopped onion	1/2 cup	125 mL
Chopped carrot	1/2 cup	125 mL
Chopped celery	1/2 cup	125 mL
All-purpose flour	1/2 cup	125 mL
Chicken broth	3 cups	375 mL
Cans of plum tomatoes (14 oz., 398 mL, each)	2	2
Cans of tomato puree (14 oz., 398 mL, each), (see page 55)	2	2
Garlic cloves, minced	2	2
Salt	2 tsp.	10 mL
Dried thyme	1 tsp.	5 mL
Pepper	1 tsp.	5 mL
Granulated sugar	2 tsp.	10 mL

Cook bacon in a large saucepan over medium heat, stirring occasionally, until crisp. Transfer to a plate lined with paper towel to drain and set aside. Drain all but 2 tbsp. (30 mL) of drippings from pan.

Add butter and heat until melted. Add onion, carrot and celery, and cook until slightly softened, about 7 to 8 minutes.

Add flour and stir to make a roux. Cook, stirring constantly, until roux is slightly brown, about 15 minutes.

Slowly add broth, whisking constantly, and bring to a boil. Stir in tomatoes and tomato puree. Bring to a boil, and then reduce heat to a simmer.

Stir in next 4 ingredients. Simmer over low heat, stirring occasionally, for about 45 minutes until sauce is reduced to desired consistency. Stir in sugar. Remove and discard bay leaf. Carefully process with an immersion blender or in a blender until smooth, following manufacturer's safety instructions for processing hot liquids. Can be stored in an airtight container in refrigerator for up to 5 days. Makes 8 cups (2 L).

Portugaise/Portuguese

This sauce is built from the tomato mother sauce to which chopped, peeled tomatoes (known as tomato *concassée*), onion and garlic are added, and the sauce is finished with chopped fresh parsley. It pairs well with fish, grilled meat and pasta dishes.

Cooking oil	1 tbsp.	15 mL
Finely chopped onion	1/4 cup	60 mL
Tomato, seeded, chopped and peeled	1 cup	250 mL
Garlic clove, minced	1	1
Tomato Sauce (see page 34)	**2 cups**	**500 mL**
Finely chopped flat leaf parsley	2 tbsp.	30 mL

Heat oil in a medium saucepan on medium. Add onion and cook until softened, about 5 minutes. Add tomatoes and garlic. Simmer until reduced to about half.

Stir in tomato sauce and bring back to a simmer. Cook for about 10 minutes to blend flavours. Remove from heat and stir in parsley. Can be stored in an airtight container in refrigerator for about 4 days. Makes about 3 cups (750 mL).

Tomato *concasée* is a French style of preparing tomatoes in which they are boiled to loosen the skins and then seeded and chopped. Removing the seeds and skin eliminates any bitterness, leaving only the natural sweetness of the tomatoes.

Espagnole Tomate/Spanish

This sauce, a spicier version of the tomato mother sauce, is enhanced with mushrooms, green pepper and chilies or hot sauce. In French cuisine, dishes given *a l'Espagnole* in the title were said to be inspired by Spanish cuisine and usually contained tomatoes, sweet peppers, onion and garlic as their main ingredients. This sauce pairs well with chicken, pork and seafood dishes.

Cooking oil	1 tbsp.	15 mL
Finely chopped onion	2/3 cup	150 mL
Thinly sliced mushrooms	3/4 cup	175 mL
Finely chopped green pepper	1/3 cup	75 mL
Garlic clove, minced	1	1
Tomato Sauce (see page 34)	**2 cups**	**500 mL**
Hot pepper sauce, optional	1 tsp.	5 mL
Salt, to taste		
Pepper, to taste		

Heat oil in a medium saucepan on medium. Add onion and cook until softened, about 5 or 6 minutes.

Stir in mushrooms and green peppers and cook for another 5 to 6 minutes.

Add garlic and cook until fragrant, 1 to 2 minutes.

Stir in tomato sauce and hot pepper sauce, if using. Season with salt and pepper. Bring to a simmer and cook for about 15 minutes, stirring occasionally. Can be stored in an airtight container in refrigerator for about 4 days. Makes about 3 1/2 cups (875 mL).

Creole

Another sauce built from the tomato mother sauce, Creole Sauce is enriched with the "holy trinity" of Creole cooking—onion, celery and green pepper. A little cayenne pepper adds a touch of heat. This sauce is served with shrimp, grilled chicken or vegetables, particularly eggplant.

Cooking oil	2 tbsp.	30 mL
Onion, finely chopped	1/3 cup	75 mL
Diced celery	1/3 cup	75 mL
Finely diced green pepper	1/3 cup	75 mL
Garlic clove, minced	1	1
Tomato Sauce (see page 34)	**2 cups**	**500 mL**
Bay leaf	1	1
Ground thyme	1/2 tsp.	2 mL
Lemon zest	1/4 tsp.	1 mL
Salt	1/2 tsp.	2 mL
Pepper	1/4 tsp.	1 mL
Ground cayenne pepper	1/4 tsp.	1 mL

Heat oil in a medium saucepan on medium. Add next 3 ingredients and cook until onion softens, about 5 to 6 minutes.

Add garlic and cook until fragrant, 1 to 2 minutes.

Stir in next 4 ingredients and bring to a simmer. Cook, stirring occasionally, for about 15 minutes. Remove and discard bay leaf.

Stir in remaining 3 ingredients. Can be stored in an airtight container in refrigerator for about 4 days. Makes about 3 cups (750 mL).

In Cajun and Creole cooking, the "holy trinity" is equivalent to the *mirepoix* in French cuisine, except where a *mirepoix* is two parts onion and one part carrot and celery, the holy trinity is equal parts of each vegetable.

Velouté

The second of the white mother sauces, Velouté, gets its name from its silky smooth consistency. *Velouté* means "velvety" or "smooth" in French. This sauce is also known as Sauce Blanche Grasse or Oily White Sauce, which doesn't seem nearly elegant enough for such an esteemed sauce. Velouté Sauce is made by simmering a white stock made from the unroasted bones of fish, chicken or veal, and thickening it with a blond roux. It can be served as is but is most often used as a base to build other sauces. The three Velouté mother sauce variations (fish, chicken and veal) have an additional three derivative sauces—White Wine Sauce from Fish Velouté, Suprême Sauce from Chicken Velouté and Allemande Sauce from Veal Velouté—that form the base for many other sauces. In North America Chicken Velouté is used much more often than Veal Velouté. Many of the sauces that were traditionally made with veal broth are now made with chicken broth.

Bay leaf	1	1
Dried thyme	1/4 tsp.	1 mL
Peppercorns, crushed	5	5
Parsley sprigs	2	2
White stock (see page 23)	5 cups	1.25 L
Butter	1/4 cup	60 mL
Diced onions	1/2 cup	125 mL
Diced celery	2 tbsp.	30 mL
All-purpose flour	1/4 cup	60 mL
Salt	1 tsp.	5 mL
White pepper	1/2 tsp.	2 mL

Wrap first 4 ingredients in a piece of cheesecloth and tie with kitchen twine to form a *bouquet garni*.

Warm stock in a medium saucepan on medium heat.

Melt butter in another medium saucepan on medium heat. Add onions and celery and cook, stirring occasionally, until softened, about 8 minutes.

Add flour and stir to combine. Turn heat to medium-low and cook, stirring frequently, to form a blond roux (see page 20), about 5 minutes. Gradually whisk in warmed stock. Whisk constantly until all stock has been used and roux has been fully incorporated with no lumps. Bring to a boil, and then reduce heat to a simmer.

Whisk in salt and white pepper. Add *bouquet garni* and stir. Cook, stirring occasionally, for 20 to 25 minutes until taste of flour has cooked away.

Strain sauce through a fine-mesh sieve or a sieve lined with cheesecloth. Discard solids and return sauce to saucepan. Bring to a simmer before serving. Sauce is best served immediately but can be stored in an airtight container in refrigerator for up to 4 days. Makes about 4 cups (1 L).

Bercy

This Bercy Sauce is essentially a white sauce version of the Bercy made with an Espagnole base. In both cases the mother sauce is enhanced with wine and shallots, but for this Bercy, the mother sauce is a Fish Velouté, and the sauce is finished with a touch of butter, parsley and a little lemon. Because of its fish base, this Bercy Sauce works especially well with fish and seafood dishes.

Fish Velouté (see page 42)	**2 cups**	**500 mL**
Finely chopped shallots	3 tbsp.	45 mL
White wine	1/2 cup	125 mL
Butter	2 tbsp.	30 mL
Finely chopped parsley	1 tbsp.	15 mL
Lemon juice	1 tsp.	5 mL

Keep velouté warm on medium-low heat.

Combine shallots and wine in a small saucepan on medium-low heat. Cook, stirring often, until reduced by two-thirds, about 5 minutes. Stir in Velouté and bring to a simmer. Cook, stirring often, until reduced by about a quarter.

Whisk in butter, parsley and lemon juice. Sauce is best served immediately but can be stored in an airtight container in refrigerator for up to 3 days. Makes about 2 cups (500 mL).

Estragon/Tarragon

There are three different tarragon sauces in French cuisine; one is a brown tarragon sauce based on Espagnole, and two are white sauces, using a Velouté as their base. This version, built from a basic Velouté, is the simpler of the two white sauces to prepare (the other version is built from a secondary sauce, Allemande, instead of a basic Velouté). We've used Fish Veloute as our base for this sauce, but it can also be made with chicken or veal, depending on what dish you plan to serve it with.

Fish Velouté (see page 42)	**4 cups**	**1. L**
Fresh tarragon leaves	2 tbsp.	30 mL
Chopped tarragon	1 tbsp.	15 mL

Keep Velouté warm on medium-low heat.

Blanch tarragon for 5 seconds in a small saucepan of boiling water. Quickly rinse and dry tarragon. Crush leaves with a mortar and pestle. Gradually mix in 1/4 cup (60 mL) of Velouté to make a paste. Stir paste into remaining

Velouté in saucepan. Bring to a simmer and cook, stirring occasionally, for about 7 minutes to allow flavours to blend. Strain sauce through a fine-mesh sieve or a sieve lined with cheesecloth, discarding solids.

Stir in chopped tarragon. Sauce is best served immediately but can be stored in an airtight container in refrigerator for up to 3 days. Makes about 4 cups (1 L).

Bercy

Normande/Normandy

Although mussel cooking liquid is traditionally used in this sauce, we've replaced it with clam juice, which can be bought commercially and therefore will save you a step in preparing this rather labour-intensive sauce. Should you prefer to adhere to tradition, substitute the same amount of mussel cooking liquid for the clam juice. Normandy Sauce is ideal to serve with fish and seafood dishes, and it also works well over pasta and vegetables such as asparagus, cauliflower and green peas.

Fish Velouté (see page 42)	**2 cups**	**500 mL**
Mushroom cooking liquid (see page 66)	**1/4 cup**	**60 mL**
Clam juice	**1/4 cup**	**60 mL**
Fish broth	**1/3 cup**	**75 mL**
Whipping cream	**1/2 cup**	**125 mL**
Egg yolks	**2**	**2**
Lemon juice	**1 tbsp.**	**15 mL**
Butter	**2 tbsp.**	**30 mL**
Salt, to taste		
Pepper, to taste		

Combine first 5 ingredients in a medium saucepan on medium. Bring to a simmer and cook, stirring occasionally, until reduced by one-third. Remove saucepan from heat.

Place egg yolks in a medium bowl. Remove 1/2 cup (125 mL) of sauce from saucepan and whisk it into egg yolks. Stir mixture back into saucepan and return saucepan to heat on medium-low. Cook, stirring constantly, until slightly thickened. Do not boil.

Whisk in lemon juice and butter. Strain sauce through a fine-mesh sieve or a sieve lined with cheesecloth, discarding solids. Season sauce with salt and pepper. Sauce is best served immediately but can be stored in an airtight container in refrigerator for up to 3 days. Makes about 3 cups (750 mL).

Vin Blanc/White Wine

This rich sauce is built from a Fish Velouté that has white wine added and is finished with butter and whipping cream. It can be served as is or used as the base to build other sauces including Chivry and Venetian. Many recipes call for dry white wine, which is rather vague. Some varieties that work well include Sauvignon Blanc and Chablis, though each has its own flavor that will influence the flavour of the sauce. Usually sweeter wines, such as Rieslings and Sauternes, as well as oaky whites such as Chardonnay are less desirable.

Fish Velouté (see page 42)	**4 cups**	**1 L**
Dry white wine	1/2 cup	125 mL
Whipping cream	1/2 cup	125 mL
Butter, cut into pieces	3 tbsp.	45 mL
Lemon juice	2 tsp.	10 mL
Salt, to taste		
White pepper, to taste		

Keep Velouté warm over medium-low heat.

Heat white wine in a medium saucepan on medium-low. Cook, stirring often, for about 5 minutes until reduced by about half. Stir in Velouté. Bring to a simmer and cook, stirring occasionally, until reduced by about half, about 12 to 15 minutes.

Meanwhile, scald cream in a small saucepan over low (see page 19). Slowly whisk cream into Velouté mixture. Remove from heat and add butter, stirring until all butter is melted.

Stir in lemon juice. Season with salt and pepper. Sauce is best served immediately but can be stored in an airtight container in refrigerator for up to 2 days. Makes about 3 cups (750 mL).

Crevettes/Shrimp

Sauce aux Crevettes (Shrimp Sauce in English) is a derivative of White Wine Sauce and, as such, has Fish Velouté as its base. It is enriched with a homemade shrimp compound butter, which we recommend you make before you start preparing the White Wine Sauce. The butter needs time to firm up before it is added to the sauce. This rich sauce is perfect for serving over pasta, potatoes or seafood dishes.

Butter, softened	1/4 cup	60 mL
Finely chopped parsley	1 tbsp.	15 mL
Lemon juice	1/2 tsp.	2 mL
White pepper	1/8 tsp.	0.5 mL
Cooked finely chopped shrimp	3 tbsp.	45 mL
White Wine Sauce (see page 48)	**2 cups**	**500 mL**
Pepper	1/4 tsp.	60 mL
Diced cooked shrimp	3 tbsp.	45 mL

Combine first 5 ingredients in a small bowl, mixing well. Transfer mixture to a sheet of parchment or wax paper and roll into a cylinder, about 1 inch (2.5 cm) thick. Chill in refrigerator until firm.

Bring White Wine Sauce to a simmer in a small saucepan on medium heat. Whisk in shrimp butter and pepper.

Remove from heat and garnish with shrimp. Sauce is best served immediately but can be stored in an airtight container in refrigerator for up to 2 days. Makes about 2 1/2 cups (625 mL).

Chivry/Herb

Traditionally Chivry Sauce was made by boiling the herb mixture in wine, straining out the herbs and adding the infused wine to a basic Velouté. The sauce was then finished by whisking in a compound herb butter. Today Chivry Sauce is usually considered a derivative of White Wine Sauce that has been enriched with the herb mixture.

Classic Chivry Sauce included salad burnet in the mix, but this herb can be difficult to find so we've left it out. If it is available in your area, by all means include it in your sauce. Chervil can also be a bit difficult to find; look for it in specialty stores or at farmers markets, especially in spring. If you can't find chervil, increase the amount of parsley instead. Chivry Sauce pairs well with fish, chicken, vegetable and egg dishes.

White Wine Sauce (see page 48)	2 cups	500 mL
Finely chopped chervil	1 tbsp.	15 mL
Finely chopped flat leaf parsley	1 tbsp.	15 mL
Finely chopped tarragon	1/2 tbsp.	7 mL
Finely chopped chives	1/2 tbsp.	7 mL

Keep White Wine Sauce warm over medium-low heat.

Add herbs to sauce, stirring gently until herbs are evenly distributed. Sauce is best served immediately but can be stored in an airtight container in refrigerator for up to 2 days. Makes 2 cups (500 mL).

Vénitienne/Venetian

This classical French herb sauce is built from White Wine Sauce to which green butter—a mixture of pureed spinach and butter—has been added. It is traditionally served with fish. We recommend making the green butter before you prepare the White Wine Sauce.

Spinach leaves, stems removed	3/4 cup	175 mL
Butter, softened	1/3 cup	75 mL
White Wine Sauce (see page 48)	2 cups	500 mL
White wine	1/4 cup	60 mL
Tarragon vinegar	1/4 cup	60 mL
Finely chopped shallots	1 tbsp.	15 mL
Finely chopped chervil	1 tsp.	5 mL
Chopped tarragon	1 tbsp.	15 mL

Steam spinach leaves until tender and wilted, about 3 minutes. Run under cold water and squeeze dry. Transfer to a small food processor or blender and process or blend until smooth. Add pureed spinach to softened butter and mix well. Chill in refrigerator until firm.

Bring White Wine Sauce to a simmer over medium-low heat.

Combine green butter and next 4 ingredients in a small saucepan on medium heat. Cook, stirring often, until reduced by two-thirds. Add White Wine Sauce and simmer for 2 to 3 minutes. Strain sauce through a fine-mesh sieve or a sieve lined with cheesecloth, discarding solids.

Stir in tarragon. Sauce is best served immediately but can be stored in an airtight container in refrigerator for up to 2 days. Makes about 2 cups (500 mL).

Chivry

Hongroise/Hungarian

Hongroise Sauce is built from a Chicken Velouté base, which is enhanced with onion, white wine and a dab of butter. The main seasoning in this sauce is paprika, hence the reference to Hungary in the name. The word "paprika" is Hungarian in origin and is the diminutive form of *papar*, meaning "pepper." Paprika wasn't introduced to Hungary until the 18th century, but the country has become one of the top producers of the spice (with 8 different varieties available ranging from sweet to pungent and mild to spicy), and paprika has become the spice that characterizes Hungarian cuisine. This sauce is a perfect accompaniment for veal, lamb poultry and eggs.

Chicken Velouté (see page 42)	**2 cups**	**500 mL**
Butter	1 tbsp.	15 mL
Finely diced onion	1/3 cup	75 mL
Paprika	2 tsp.	10 mL
White wine	1/3 cup	75 mL

Keep Velouté warm on medium-low heat.

Melt butter in a small saucepan on medium-low heat. Add onions and paprika and cook until soft, about 5 minutes.

Add wine and cook, stirring often, until reduced by half. Stir in Velouté and bring to a simmer. Cook, stirring often, for 10 minutes to allow flavours to blend. Strain through a fine-mesh sieve or a sieve lined with cheesecloth, discarding solids. Sauce is best served immediately but can be stored in an airtight container in refrigerator for up to 3 days. Makes 2 cups (500 mL).

Aurore/Aurora

This sauce is named for its colour, the result of mixing tomato puree into the creamy white Velouté. *Aurore* is the French word for "dawn," and the reddish-pink hue of this sauce is reminiscent of the sky at sunrise. Aurore Sauce is most often made with Chicken Velouté in North America, but it can also be made with a Fish Velouté or Veal Velouté base. It is delicious on vegetables, chicken, fish and eggs.

Chicken Velouté (see page 42)	**2 cups**	**500 mL**
Tomato puree (see page 55)	1/3 cup	75 mL

Keep Velouté warm on medium-low heat.

Stir tomato puree into Velouté and bring to a simmer. Cook, stirring constantly, for about 5 minutes to allow flavours to blend. Sauce is best served immediately but can be stored in an airtight container in refrigerator for up to 3 days. Makes about 2 cups (500 mL).

Tomato puree differs from crushed tomatoes in its texture. Crushed tomatoes are a slightly chunkier mix of crushed tomato pieces and tomato puree, whereas tomato puree is a blended product that is smoother and thicker than crushed tomatoes. Think of tomato puree as the mid-point between crushed tomatoes and tomato paste.

Hongroise

Currie/Curry

Escoffier believed that authentic Indian curry sauces were "not suitable for European tastes," but that the French version of curry sauce should be "generally acceptable." This sauce is extremely versatile and is delicious spooned over poultry, veal, fish, eggs and vegetables. It can be made with Fish Velouté or Veal Velouté as well, but Chicken Velouté is more traditional.

Chicken Velouté (see page 42)	**1 cup**	**250 mL**
Butter	2 tbsp.	30 mL
Finely diced onion	1/4 cup	60 mL
Finely diced celery	3 tbsp.	45 mL
Finely diced carrot	3 tbsp.	45 mL
Parsley springs	2	2
Garlic clove, minced	1	1
Curry powder	1/2 tbsp.	7 mL
Ground thyme	1/2 tsp.	2 mL
Bay leaf	1	1
Coconut milk	1 cup	250 mL
Whipping cream	1/4 cup	60 mL
Lemon juice	1 tsp.	5 mL
Salt	1/2 tsp.	2 mL
Pepper	1/2 tsp.	2 mL

Keep Velouté warm on medium-low heat.

Heat butter in a medium saucepan on medium. Add next 3 ingredients and cook, stirring occasionally, until onions are soft.

Add next 5 ingredients and cook, stirring constantly, until fragrant, about 1 minute.

Stir in Velouté and coconut milk and bring to a simmer. Cook, stirring occasionally, for 20 minutes to allow flavours to blend.

Stir in whipping cream. Strain sauce through a fine-mesh sieve or a sieve lined with cheesecloth, discarding solids. Stir in remaining 3 ingredients. Sauce is best served immediately but can be stored in an airtight container in refrigerator for up to 3 days. Makes about 3 cups (750 mL).

Suprême/Supreme

Suprême Sauce is another example of a secondary or small sauce that is used as a foundation for building even more sauces (Champignon, Albufera and Ivory, to name a few). Suprême Sauce is made by enriching Chicken Velouté with cream and butter, and it is delicious served as a sauce in its own right. It can be thought of as the poultry version of White Wine Sauce and is ideal for serving with sautéed or poached chicken as well as roasted or grilled vegetables such as broccoli, peppers, cauliflowers and asparagus.

Chicken Velouté (see page 42)	**4 cups**	**1 L**
Whipping cream	1 cup	250 mL
Butter	2 tbsp.	30 mL
Salt, to taste		
White pepper, to taste		

Simmer Velouté on medium heat, stirring occasionally, until reduced to about a quarter.

Pour whipping cream into a heatproof bowl. Slowly stir 1/4 cup (60 mL) of Velouté into cream (see Tip, below). Stir cream mixture slowly back into sauce in saucepan. Return sauce to a simmer.

Whisk in butter and season with salt and pepper. Sauce is best served immediately but can be stored in an airtight container in refrigerator for up to 3 days. Makes about 2 cups (500 mL).

Tip: When adding dairy products or eggs to a warm sauce, it is a good idea to temper the sauce to ensure that the dairy products don't curdle and the eggs don't cook. Remove a small portion of the sauce and stir it into the dairy product or beaten eggs you want to add, stirring until smooth. Slowly add this mixture back to the sauce in your saucepan and warm it gently. Do not overheat or bring to a boil or the sauce can curdle or break.

Champignon/Mushroom

For this sauce, Suprême Sauce is enriched with mushrooms that have been sautéed in butter. Lemon juice is added to the mushrooms to prevent them from browning as they cook. This sauce is best served with poultry or veal dishes.

Suprême Sauce (see page 58)	**2 cups**	**500 mL**
Butter	1 1/2 tbsp.	7 mL
Thinly sliced mushrooms	2/3 cup	150 mL
Lemon juice	2 tsp.	10 mL

Keep Suprême Sauce warm on medium-low heat.

Melt butter in a small frying pan on medium heat. Add mushrooms and lemon juice and cook, stirring often, for 4 to 5 minutes until mushrooms are softened. Stir mushrooms into sauce. Sauce is best served immediately but can be stored in an airtight container in refrigerator for up to 3 days. Makes about 2 cups (500 mL).

Ivoire/Ivory

Sauce Ivoire, or Ivory Sauce, gets its name from the colour it takes on once the *glace de viande* is stirred into the Suprême Sauce. *Glace de viande*, or meat glaze, is brown stock that has been reduced until it becomes thick and syrupy. Because it is so concentrated, *glace de viande* has an intense flavour that adds real depth to soups, stews, sauces or whatever it is added to. With Ivory Sauce, the result is a creamy, savoury delight that is excellent over poached eggs and poultry.

Suprême Sauce (see page 58)	**2 cups**	**500 mL**
Glace de viande (see below)	1 1/2 tbsp.	22 mL

Keep Suprême Sauce warm on medium-low heat.

Stir *glace de viande* into Suprême Sauce until incorporated. Bring to a simmer and cook for about 10 minutes to blend flavours. Sauce is best served immediately but can be stored in an airtight container in refrigerator for up to 3 days. Makes about 2 cups (500 mL).

To make *glace de viande*, or meat glaze, bring 16 cups (4 L) of beef stock (not broth) to a slow simmer for about 45 minutes, skimming the top of the stock every 10 minutes or so, until reduced by half. Strain stock through a fine-mesh sieve or a sieve lined with cheesecloth, discarding solids. Pour stock into a small saucepan and continue to simmer, skimming the top as needed, until reduced to about half. The glaze is ready when it coats the back of a spoon and has the consistency of liquid honey. Remove from heat and set aside to cool. Store in a glass jar with a tight-fitting lid in the refrigerator for about 1 month. Makes about 3/4 cup (175 mL).

Albufera

Antoine Carême is believed to have created this sauce and named it in honour of Louis Gabriel Suchet, a general in Napoleon's army who led his soldiers to victory against Spanish forces in a battle for Valencia during the Peninsular War. For his efforts, Suchet was bestowed the title of Duc D'Albufera (Albufera being the name of a freshwater lagoon in Valencia, which is now a National Park). It is not clear whether Carême's sauce included the red pepper butter, but Escoffier's later version of this sauce did. Albufera Sauce is usually served with poultry.

Suprême Sauce (see page 58)	**2 cups**	**500 mL**
Butter, softened	1/4 cup	60 mL
Finely chopped roasted red peppers	3 tbsp.	45 mL
Salt	1/4 tsp.	1 mL
Glace de viande (see p. 61)	1/3 cup	75 mL

Keep Suprême Sauce warm on medium-low heat.

Combine next 3 ingredients in a small bowl, mixing well. Transfer mixture to a sheet of parchment or wax paper and roll into a cylinder, about 1 inch (2.5 cm) thick. Chill in refrigerator until firm.

Combine Suprême Sauce and *glace de viande* in a small saucepan on medium-low heat. Add half of roasted red pepper butter, reserving other half for future use. Stir until butter has melted and is incorporated into sauce. Sauce is best served immediately but can be stored in an airtight container in refrigerator for up to 3 days. Makes about 2 1/2 cups (625 mL).

Bonnefoy

This sauce is sometimes called Sauce Bordelaise au Vin Blanc, or White Bordelaise Sauce, because it is essentially the white wine version of Bordelaise Sauce except that it has a Veal Velouté base instead of an Espagnole base. It is a rich sauce that goes well with roasted chicken or turkey, veal and grilled fish. The name Bonnefoy is most likely a tip of the hat to the Bonnefoy restaurant, a famous French restaurant in 19th-century Paris.

White wine	2 cups	500 mL
Shallots, finely chopped	1/4 cup	60 mL
Pepper	1 tsp.	5 mL
Bay leaf	1	1
Sprig of thyme	1	1
Veal Velouté (see page 42)	**1 cup**	**250 mL**
Chopped tarragon	1 tbsp.	15 mL
Lemon juice	2 tsp.	10 mL

Combine first 5 ingredients in a medium saucepan on medium heat and bring to a simmer. Cook, stirring occasionally, until mixture has reduced to 1/2 cup (125 mL).

Whisk in Velouté and bring to a simmer. Cook, stirring occasionally, for about 15 minutes to allow flavours to blend. Strain through a fine-mesh sieve or a sieve lined with cheesecloth, discarding solids.

Stir in tarragon and lemon juice. Sauce is best served immediately but can be stored in an airtight container in refrigerator for up to 3 days. Makes about 1 1/2 cups (375 mL).

Horseradish

This rich, creamy sauce has a nice kick thanks to the horseradish. It is great served over beef, especially a juicy steak.

Veal Velouté (see page 42)	**2 cups**	**500 mL**
Prepared horseradish	3 tbsp.	45 mL
Whipping cream	1/4 cup	60 mL
Dry mustard	1 tsp.	5 mL
White wine vinegar	1 tbsp.	15 mL

Keep Velouté warm on medium-low heat.

Combine next 4 ingredients in a small bowl, mixing well. Slowly stir 2 tbsp. (30 mL) of Velouté into mixture (see Tip, page 58). Stir mixture back into Velouté in saucepan. Cook, stirring constantly, until heated through. Sauce is best served immediately but can be stored in an airtight container in refrigerator for up to 3 days. Makes 2 cups (500 mL).

Bonnefoy

Villageoise

This sauce can be time consuming because you have to make so many of the ingredients: the white stock, the mushroom cooking liquid and the Soubise Sauce. For a simpler version, omit the Soubise Sauce and add sautéed, finely chopped onions at the end to finish the sauce. Villageoise Sauce is classically made with Veal Velouté, but Chicken Velouté can be used as well. This sauce is excellent served with white meat, poultry or vegetables such as asparagus and broccoli.

White stock (see page 23)	1/4 cup	60 mL
Mushroom cooking liquid (see below)	1/4 cup	60 mL
Veal Velouté (see page 42)	**1 1/2 cups**	**375 mL**
Soubise sauce (see page 16)	1/2 cups	125 mL
Egg yolks (large)	2	2
Butter	3 1/2 tbsp.	52 mL
Whipping cream	1/3 cup	75 mL

Combine first 3 ingredients in a medium saucepan on medium heat. Cook until reduce to about 1 1/2 cups (375 mL). Strain through a fine-mesh sieve or a sieve lined with cheesecloth, discarding solids. Return sauce to saucepan on medium-low heat.

Whisk in Soubise Sauce.

Beat egg yolks in a heat-resistant bowl. Slowly stir in 1/2 cup (125 mL) of warm sauce from saucepan. Slowly stir egg mixture back into saucepan. Whisk in butter until well combined.

Thin sauce with whipping cream to desired consistency. You may not use entire amount of cream if you prefer a thicker sauce. Sauce is best served immediately but can be stored in an airtight container in refrigerator for up to 3 days. Makes about 3 cups (750 mL).

✿ To make mushroom cooking liquid, combine 1 1/2 cups (375 mL) chopped cremini mushrooms and 2 cups (500 mL) water in a small pot on medium heat. Bring to a simmer and cook, covered, for 15 minutes. Strain through a fine-mesh sieve, discarding solids. Set liquid aside to cool. Store in an airtight container in refrigerator for up to 2 weeks. Makes about 1 1/2 cups (375 mL).

Allemande

Under Antoine Carême, Allemande enjoyed the status of one of the mother sauces, but Escoffier demoted it to a secondary sauce in the Velouté group. Allemande Sauce is made by thickening Veal Velouté with a liaison of egg yolks and whipping cream. The end result is a rich, creamy, "blond" sauce that gets its name from the French word for "German." Some food historians suggest that the sauce's name was based on the French generalization that most German people had blond hair. Regardless of its origin, this sauce's name, like Espagnole, was controversial in 19th-century France and was disparaged as being unpatriotic. France and Germany were involved in many conflicts at the time, and France had been defeated in the Franco-Prussian war, so public sentiment in France was decidedly cool towards Germany. There was a move to change the name of the sauce to Sauce Parisienne, which caught on with some chefs, but today, Parisienne Sauce generally refers to a sauce that uses cream cheese as a liaison.

Veal Velouté (see page 42)	**4 cups**	**1 L**
Egg yolks (large)	2	2
Whipping cream	1/2 cup	125 mL
Lemon juice	1 1/2 tsp.	7 mL
Salt	1/2 tsp.	2 mL
White pepper	1/4 tsp.	1 mL

Simmer Velouté in a medium saucepan on medium, stirring occasionally, until slightly reduced, about 7 to 8 minutes.

Beat egg yolks and cream in a heat-resistant bowl. Slowly add 2/3 cup (150 mL) Velouté to egg yolk mixture, stirring constantly. Slowly add mixture to sauce in saucepan, stirring constantly. Bring back to just below a simmer. Do not boil.

Whisk in lemon juice, salt and white pepper. Strain in a fine-mesh sieve or a sieve lined with cheesecloth, discarding solids. Sauce is best served immediately but can be stored in an airtight container in refrigerator for up to 3 days. Makes about 4 cups (1 L).

Allemande Sauce, strictly speaking, should be made with Veal Velouté, but in North America it is more often made with Chicken Velouté.

Poulette

Although this sauce is a derivative of Allemande Sauce, and therefore has Fish Velouté as its base, it is named after a hen. Specifically, the French word *poulette* translates to "pullet," meaning a hen that is less than one year old. We can only assume that this sauce was named for what it pairs best with rather than what it contains. Poulette Sauce is generally served with grilled chicken and other poultry dishes, though it also works well drizzled over roasted and grilled vegetables.

Allemande Sauce (see page 66)	**2 cups**	**500 mL**
Butter	1 tbsp.	15 mL
Thinly sliced mushrooms	1 cup	250 mL
Finely chopped parsley	1 tbsp.	15 mL
Lemon juice	2 tsp.	10 mL

Keep Allemande Sauce warm on medium-low heat.

Melt butter in a medium saucepan on medium heat. Add mushrooms and cook, stirring often, until soft, about 5 minutes. Whisk in Allemande Sauce and bring to a simmer. Simmer for about 10 minutes, stirring occasionally, to allow flavours to combine.

Stir in parsley and lemon juice. Sauce is best served immediately but can be stored in an airtight container in refrigerator for up to 3 days. Makes about 2 cups (500 mL).

Estragon/Tarragon

Although it shares its name with the Estragon Sauce made from Fish Velouté , it is a much more elaborate sauce than its namesake. This sauce is a derivative of Allemande Sauce that has been enriched with tarragon butter and lemon. It is delicious served with poultry and veal dishes. The tarragon butter must be prepared in advance so it has time to chill thoroughly before being added to the sauce.

Tarragon leaves	3 tbsp.	45 mL
Butter, softened	1/3 cup	75 mL
Allemande Sauce (see page 66)	**2 cups**	**500 mL**
Lemon juice	2 tsp.	10 mL
Chopped tarragon leaves	1 tbsp.	15 mL

Blanch tarragon leaves for 5 seconds in boiling salted water. Rinse and dry well. Process with a mortar and pestle until leaves form a fine paste.

Combine paste and butter in a small bowl, mixing well. Transfer mixture to a sheet of parchment or wax paper and roll into a cylinder, about 1 inch (2.5 cm) thick. Chill in refrigerator until firm. Cut into pieces and keep cold.

Warm Allemande Sauce in a medium saucepan on medium-low heat until it just begins to simmer. Whisk cold tarragon butter in, 1 piece at a time, until all is incorporated.

Whisk in lemon juice and chopped tarragon leaves. Sauce is best served immediately but can be stored in an airtight container in refrigerator for up to 3 days. Makes about 2 1/4 cups (550 mL).

Poulette

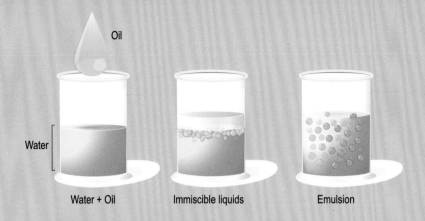

Water + Oil   Immiscible liquids   Emulsion

Emulsified Sauces

Emulsification is the process by which two immiscible liquids (liquids that cannot dissolve into each other) are combined to form a stable solution, with one liquid suspended in the other. In an emulsion, small droplets of one liquid (called the **dispersed liquid**) are distributed throughout the other liquid (called the **continuous liquid**). There are two types of emulsions: one in which water droplets are suspended in oil or fat (e.g. butter), and the other in which oil or fat droplets are suspended in water (e.g. mayonnaise).

You can achieve a temporary emulsion by whisking or vigorously shaking the liquids together, which breaks the dispersed liquid into tiny droplets that can float in the continuous liquid, but the emulsion will not last long before the liquids separate back into layers.

For an emulsion to have staying power, the droplets of the dispersed liquid must be kept separate from each other, or else they will stick together, and the emulsion will separate.

To keep the droplets apart, you need an **emulsifier**. Emulsifiers work in two ways: first, they coat the droplets, preventing them from sticking to each other. Second, they have molecules with one part that is hydrophilic (water loving) and one part that is hydrophobic (water hating). The hydrophilic part attracts the water droplets and the hydrophobic part attracts the oil, stabilizing the solution.

Emulsions are thicker than either of the liquids that are combined to make it, which is perfect for making rich, creamy sauces.

Saving a Broken Sauce

It can be devastating when the sauce you've carefully coaxed together
from its base ingredients separates into a disappointing mess of liquid
and fat. When this happens, the sauce is said to have "broken." If a sauce
is breaking, you'll notice little droplets of oil forming around the edges.
Obviously you can't serve your broken sauce to your dinner guests (it
would be a grainy mess), but don't worry. All is not lost! There are a few
ways to (potentially) save a broken sauce. The method you choose depends
on the type of sauce and why it is breaking.

• For a cold sauce, like mayonnaise, try processing the sauce in a blender,
  which will break the dispersed liquid down into smaller droplets.

• For a cooked sauce that has been overheated, try whisking in a spoonful
  or two of cool water.

• For a cooked sauce that seems a bit thin and is breaking, try adding a little
  more fat, such as butter or an egg yolk, and whisk constantly until the
  sauce emulsifies again.

• If your sauce breaks because it has been sitting around too long, try
  re-warming it slowly while whisking it constantly.

Classic Hollandaise

Although he did not call it such, La Varenne had a basic version of Hollandaise sauce in his 1651 cookbook, *Le Cuisinier François*. The history of the version we are familiar with today is murky. One school of thought suggests that the classic French sauce is actually an adaptation of a Dutch sauce, hence the name Hollandaise. Another school of thought suggests that the sauce is French in origin but was given its name to honour Holland, which was renowned for the quality of its butter and eggs. This sauce is classically served over eggs benedict, asparagus and fish. It is made with clarified butter because the sauce would be too thin if whole butter was used. Do not serve it over very hot food or the sauce can break. Instead serve it over warm food or on the side for hot food.

Black peppercorns, crushed	9	9
White wine vinegar	3 tbsp.	45 mL
Water	1 1/2 tbsp.	22 mL
Egg yolks (large), room temperature	3	3
Fresh lemon juice	1 tbsp.	15 mL
Clarified butter, warmed (see page 75)	1 cup	250 mL
Fresh lemon juice	1 tbsp.	15 mL
Salt, to taste		
Ground white pepper, to taste		
Ground cayenne pepper, to taste		

Combine first 3 ingredients in a small saucepan on medium-low heat. Cook, stirring occasionally, until reduced by half.

Place egg yolks in top pot of a double boiler. Strain vinegar mixture through a fine-mesh sieve into yolks. Place pot over bottom pot of double boiler on medium-low heat. Heat mixture, whipping constantly, until yolks begin to thicken, about 3 to 5 minutes. Mixture is thick enough when it coats the back of a spoon and you can draw a line through it. Do not overcook yolks. Remove top pot from double boiler.

To stop yolks from continuing to cook, immediately whisk in first amount of lemon juice.

Slowly whisk in warm clarified butter, a few teaspoons at a time. Once eggs begin to emulsify, you can add remaining butter more quickly, whisking constantly, until all butter is incorporated.

Whisk in second amount of lemon juice, salt, pepper and cayenne. Serve immediately. This sauce cannot be stored or reheated. Makes 1 1/2 cups (375 mL).

Although you can make Hollandaise sauce with whole regular butter, your sauce will be more stable and consistent if you use clarified butter. To make 1 cup (250 mL) of clarified butter, melt 1 1/4 cups (300 mL) of cut up butter in a heavy-bottomed saucepan over medium-low heat. Do not stir. Skim the foam from the surface. Strain the clear melted butter through a fine-mesh strainer lined with cheesecloth, leaving the milky liquid at the bottom of the saucepan. Store the clarified butter in the refrigerator in a glass jar with a lid for up to six months. Do not let any water get into the jar as it can cause bacteria growth and spoil the clarified butter.

Blender Hollandaise

If you don't have time to make the classic Hollandaise Sauce, this quick, easy sauce is a great substitute.

Egg yolks (large)	4	4
Lemon juice	2 tbsp.	30 mL
Ground cayenne pepper, to taste		
Salt, to taste		
Butter	1 cup	250 mL

Process first 4 ingredients in a blender for 5 to 7 seconds until smooth.

Melt butter in a small saucepan. With blender motor running, slowly pour butter through hole in lid, processing until thick and fluffy. Serve immediately or keep warm for up to 30 minutes in top of a double boiler or in a medium bowl set on a saucepan over simmering water. This sauce does not store or reheat well. Makes 1 1/3 cups (325 mL).

Maltaise

Thanks to the addition of orange juice in place of lemon, Maltaise Sauce is a bit sweeter and tangier than regular Hollandaise. It is meant to be prepared with blood oranges, which give the sauce a subtle reddish tint, but navel oranges will work too if blood oranges are not in season. In traditional French cuisine, this sauce is served over asparagus, but it is also wonderful over other green vegetables such as broccoli and green beans. In the past, blood oranges were also known as Malta oranges, hence the name of this sauce.

Hollandaise Sauce (see page 74)	1 1/2 cups	375 mL
Fresh blood orange juice	3 tbsp.	45 mL
Orange zest (see Tip, page 108)	1 tsp.	5 mL

Whisk orange juice and zest into warm Hollandaise Sauce. Serve immediately or keep warm for up to 30 minutes in top of a double boiler or in a medium bowl set on a saucepan over simmering water. This sauce does not store or reheat well. Makes about 1 3/4 cups (425 mL).

Maltaise

Mousseline

Adding whipped cream to Hollandaise Sauce results in the incredibly rich, luxurious yet delicate Mousseline Sauce. Before adding the whipped cream, allow the Hollandaise to cool slightly, and fold the whipped cream gently into the sauce. A heavy hand will result in a heavier sauce instead of the airy delight Mousseline is meant to be. Also, add the whipped cream just before serving or the cream will lose its fluffiness and release water into the sauce.

Hollandaise Sauce (see page 74)	**1 1/2 cups**	**375 mL**
Whipping cream	**1/2 cup**	**125 mL**

Remove Hollandaise Sauce from heat and allow to cool slightly.

Whip cream until stiff peaks form. Fold into Hollandaise Sauce. Serve immediately. This sauce does not store or reheat well. Makes 2 cups (500 mL).

This sauce is also known as Chantilly Sauce, named for Chantilly cream, a vanilla-infused whipped cream that features prominently in French pastries and desserts. It pairs well with fish, delicate vegetables and eggs.

Divine

This light, airy sauce is similar to Mousseline Sauce except that the whipping cream is infused with sherry before it is added to the Hollandaise. It has a stronger flavour than Mousseline and pairs especially well with chicken and fish.

Hollandaise Sauce (see page 74)	**1 1/2 cups**	**375 mL**
Dry sherry	**1/2 cup**	**125 mL**
Whipping cream	**1/2 cup**	**125 mL**

Keep Hollandaise Sauce warm on medium-low heat.

In a small saucepan on medium heat reduce sherry down to about 3 tbsp. (45 mL). Set aside to cool. Remove Hollandaise Sauce from heat and allow it to cool slightly.

Whip cream until stiff peaks form. Fold sherry reduction into whipped cream until well incorporated. Fold sherry-infused whipped cream into Hollandaise Sauce. Serve immediately. This sauce does not store or reheat well. Makes about 2 cups (500 mL).

Mousseline

Classic Béarnaise

This classic sauce is much like an herbed Hollandaise. The cooking method for both sauces is the same, but Béarnaise gets its unique flavour from the addition of shallots, tarragon and chervil. Credit for this sauce usually goes to chef Jules Collinet, who created it for the 1836 opening of Le Pavillon Henri IV, a restaurant near Paris. He named it in honour of Henri IV, *béarnaise* meaning "from Béarne," a province in the French Pyrenees where Henri IV was born. This sauce is usually served over grilled meat, fish or eggs, and is often served with chateaubriand. As with Hollandaise, Béarnaise should not be served over hot food, or the sauce will break. If it breaks, it can sometimes be saved by whisking in a few drops of cold water.

Finely chopped shallots	2 tbsp.	30 mL
Finely chopped fresh tarragon	3 tbsp.	45 mL
Finely chopped fresh chervil	1 1/2 tbsp.	22 mL
Coarsely ground pepper	1 tsp.	5 mL
White wine vinegar	1/2 cup	125 mL
Egg yolks (large), room temperature	3	3
Fresh lemon juice	1 tbsp.	15 mL
Clarified butter, warmed (see Tip, page 75)	1 cup	250 mL
Lemon juice	1 tbsp.	15 mL
Salt, to taste		
Ground white pepper, to taste		
Ground cayenne pepper, to taste		
Chopped fresh tarragon	1 tbsp	15 mL

Combine first 5 ingredients in a small saucepan on medium-low. Cook, stirring often, until reduced to about half. Set aside to cool slightly.

Place egg yolks into a stainless steel bowl. Strain vinegar reduction into yolks. Place bowl over a double boiler on medium-low heat. Whip yolk mixture constantly until yolks start to thicken, about 3 to 5 minutes. Do not overcook. Remove bowl from double boiler.

To stop yolks from continuing to cook, immediately whisk in first amount of lemon juice.

Slowly add in butter a few teaspoons at a time, whisking constantly. Once eggs begin to emulsify, butter may be added more quickly. Continue to add butter until it is all incorporated.

Whisk in second amount of lemon juice and adjust seasonings to taste. Garnish with tarragon. Serve immediately. This sauce does not store or reheat well. Makes 1 1/2 cups (375 mL).

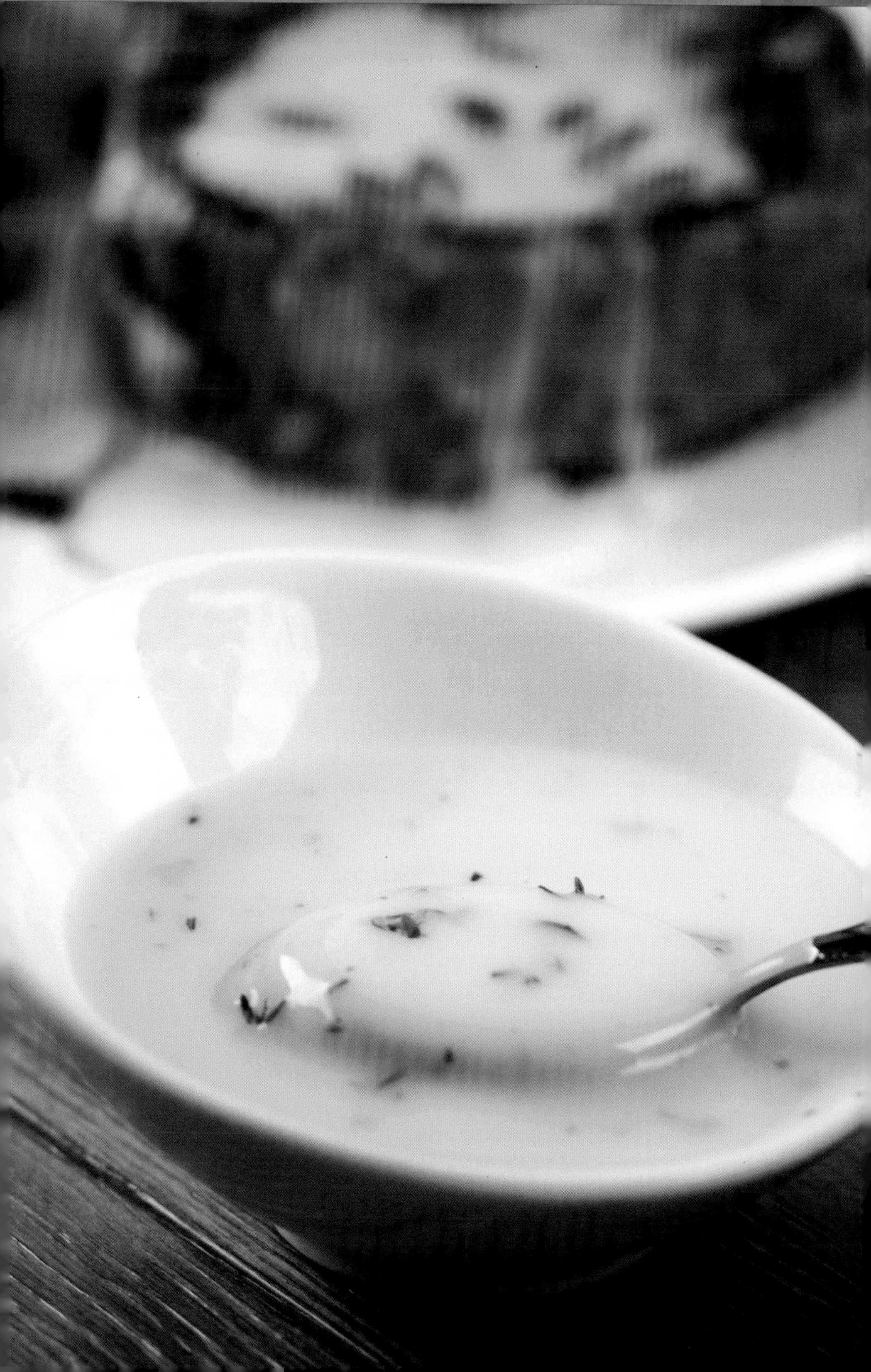

Creamy Béarnaise

Classic sauce purists would no doubt be appalled at the thought of preparing a sauce in the microwave, but this simplified version of Béarnaise has the same great taste of the original version with much less effort and room for error.

Butter, melted	1/4 cup	60 mL
Minced onion	1 tsp.	5 mL
White wine vinegar	1 tbsp.	15 mL
Egg yolks (large), lightly beaten	2	2
Whole cream (30%)	2 tbsp.	30 mL
Lemon juice	1 tsp.	5 mL
Chopped fresh parsley (or tarragon, or a combination of both)	1 tsp.	5 mL
Salt	1/4 tsp.	1 mL
Dry mustard	1/4 tsp.	1 mL

Pour melted butter into a medium microwave-safe bowl and stir in onion, white wine vinegar, egg yolks, cream and lemon juice.

Season with parsley, salt and dry mustard. Place bowl in microwave and cook until thickened and smooth, 1 to 2 minutes, stirring every 30 seconds. Serve immediately. This sauce does not store or reheat well. Makes 3/4 cup (175 mL).

Choron

Also called Sauce Béarnaise Tomatée, Choron Sauce is a Béarnaise to which tomato paste has been added. It is best served with grilled meats and poultry. This sauce can also be made with a tomato *concassé* (see page 36) or finely diced seeded tomatoes but the end result will be chunky, not smooth. Even though it is considered a derivative of Béarnaise, classic Choron Sauce, according to Escoffier and his followers, should not contain the chopped tarragon and chervil that flavours Béarnaise.

Tomato paste (see Tip, below)	2 tbsp.	30 mL
Béarnaise sauce (see page 80)	**1 1/2 cups**	**375 mL**

Whisk tomato paste into Béarnaise sauce. Serve immediately. This sauce does not store or reheat well. Makes about 1 1/2 cups (375 mL).

Tip: If a recipe calls for less than an entire can of tomato paste, freeze the unopened can for 30 minutes. Open both ends and push the contents through one end. Slice off only what you need. Freeze the remaining paste in a resealable freezer bag or plastic wrap for future use.

Choron

Mayonnaise

Popular history suggests that Mayonnaise, originally called Mahonaisse, was created in Mahon, Spain, in 1756 for a celebration dinner honouring the capture of the city for France by the Duc de Richelieu. This origin story has been disputed though, with another school of thought suggesting that Carême deserves the credit as inventor for his sauce, which he called Magnonnaise. This theory suggests that he named his sauce for the French word *manier*, meaning "to stir," because the sauce required so much stirring to emulsify. Whatever the origin, this sauce has achieved near global popularity, both on its own and as a base for other dishes.

Egg yolks (large)	2	2
White wine vinegar	4 tsp.	20 mL
Dry mustard	1/2 tbsp.	7 mL
Ground white pepper	1/2 tsp.	2 mL
Salt	1 tsp.	5 mL
Vegetable oil	2 cups	500 mL
Lemon juice	2 tbsp.	30 mL
Water	1 tbsp.	15 mL

Combine egg yolks and vinegar in a medium bowl, whisking until slightly foamy.

In a separate bowl, whisk dry mustard, white pepper and salt into oil until well combined. Gradually pour oil to egg mixture in a thin stream, whisking constantly. As mixture begins to thicken, slowly add lemon juice to thin it out. If mixture is still too thick, whisk in water.

Store in an airtight container for up to 5 days. Makes 2 cups (500 mL).

If you would prefer to make this sauce in a blender, process the first 2 ingredients until combined. In a bowl, combine the seasonings and oil. With the blender on low speed, slowly add the seasoned oil until mixture is thickened. Add the lemon juice, and thin with water, if necessary.

Aioli

Although we generally think of Aioli as a garlicky version of Mayonnaise, Aioli predates mayo by at least 1600 years. Pliny the Elder of ancient Rome mentions an emulsified sauce made of olive oil and garlic, called *Aleatum*, that was popular but tricky to make. In Catalonia, where Pliny lived as a procurator when it was part of the Roman Empire, there has long been an emulsified sauce made of garlic, olive oil and salt, called *Allioli*. This sauce seems to have spread throughout much of the Mediterranean. At some point egg yolks were added to help with the emulsification, and Aioli as we know it today was born—though for convenience the sauce is generally made with a mayonnaise base today.

Garlic cloves, minced	9	9
Lemon juice	2 tbsp.	30 mL
Mayonnaise (see page 84)	**1 cup**	**250 mL**
Olive oil	1 tbsp.	15 mL
Salt	1/2 tsp.	2 mL
Pepper	1/2 tsp.	2 mL

Combine garlic and lemon juice in a medium bowl. Let stand for about 15 minutes.

Whisk in mayonnaise, olive oil, salt and pepper. Let stand at room temperature for at least 30 minutes before serving. Store in an airtight container in refrigerator for up to 5 days. Makes about 1 cup (250 mL).

Remoulade

The origin of this sauce is unclear, but it appeared in André Viard's influential culinary cookbook/encyclopedia, *Le Cuisinier Impérial,* published in 1807. Viard was a renowned chef in his time, and his cookbook was one of the two most popular cookbooks during much of the 19th century (the other being Carème's *Le Cuisinier Parisiene: ou l'art de la cuisine Française au dix-neuvième siècle).* From France, this sauce spread throughout much of Europe and then around the world, though different countries have created their own variations. It was traditionally served with meats, fish or seafood, but it is also great as a dipping sauce for fries, as a sandwich topping, basically anywhere you want a touch of something creamy.

Mayonnaise (see page 84)	**2 cups**	**500 mL**
Finely diced onion	1/4 cup	60 mL
Grainy mustard	2 tbsp.	30 mL
Chopped fresh parsley	2 tbsp.	30 mL
Hot sauce	2 tbsp.	30 mL
Chopped gherkins	1/4 cup	60 mL
Roughly chopped capers	1 tbsp.	15 mL
Lemon juice	1 tbsp.	15 mL
Salt, to taste		
Pepper, to taste		

Combine all ingredients in a blender and store in airtight container in refrigerator for 3 to 5 days. Makes 3 cups (750 mL).

Tartare/Tartar

Although Tartar Sauce is often linked with fish and chips, a classic English dish, the sauce itself is French in origin and is closely related to Remoulade. Versions of Tartar Sauce can be found in cookbooks dating back to the mid-19th century, though the origin of the name is unclear. Some have suggested that it refers to the Tartars, a Turkish-speaking people from central Eurasia, but the connection between Tartar Sauce and the Tartars people is vague at best. Perhaps a more plausible explanation is that "tartar" is a corruption of "tarator," a tangy Middle Eastern tahini-based herb sauce that is served as an accompaniment for fish and seafood dishes. Proponents of this theory suggest that Tartar Sauce is a French adaptation of the Middle Eastern sauce.

Mayonnaise (see page 84)	**1 cup**	**250 mL**
Finely chopped dill pickles	3 tbsp.	45 mL
Finely chopped capers, optional	2 tbsp.	30 mL
Dijon mustard	2 tbsp.	30 mL
Lemon juice	2 tbsp.	30 mL
Chopped fresh dill	2 tsp.	10 mL
Pepper	1 tsp.	5 mL

Whisk all 7 ingredients in a small bowl until combined. Chill, covered, for at least 1 hour before serving. Store in an airtight container in refrigerator for up to 5 days. Makes about 1 1/2 cups (375 mL).

Italian Cuisine:
A Historical Perspective

Italian cuisine can be traced back to the days of ancient Rome. At its peak, the Roman Empire covered a vast area of Europe, Asia and northern Africa. As the Romans moved into new areas, they incorporated the locally available foods into their cuisine. Some of the main foods of ancient Rome—olive oil, wine, bread, legumes, cheese—are still staples in Italy.

Apicius, a Roman gourmand made famous for his cookbook of recipes that is thought to date back to the 1st century CE, mentions many sauces, most of which were used to season meat. Many of the herbs and spices used in those recipes, including dill, fennel, oregano, marjoram, pepper and cumin, are still popular today. The most common liquid ingredients in ancient Roman sauces were oil, garum or liquamen (see page 171), honey, milk, fruit juice or water. The sauces were often thickened with crumbled bread or pastry.

It's difficult to trace the history of Italian cuisine after the fall of the Roman Empire because little has been recorded. In the time between the end of the Roman Empire and the unification of Italy in 1861, the area was invaded and/or conquered by many different groups including the Visigoths, the Huns, the Spanish, the French, the Normans and the Arabs. Each of these other cultures influenced Italian cuisine with new ingredients and techniques.

Take pasta as an example. The Chinese, Italians and Arabs have all been credited with creating pasta. For years the common belief was that Marco Polo introduced pasta to Italy, but this theory has been largely debunked. Although noodles have been part of Chinese cuisine since antiquity (the earliest known example of noodles was unearthed from a tomb in China that dates to 4000 BCE), the noodles were made of millet, not wheat. The ancient Romans had a flat fresh pasta sheet, called *laganae*, that they layered with sauce and baked in an oven, rather like modern day lasagna, or cut into strips and added to soup. Nomadic Arabic tribes are credited with being the first to make a dried noodle, similar to modern day spaghetti, that could keep indefinitely and be easily transported, then rehydrated when it was time to eat. The Arabs introduced their dried noodles to Italy in the 9th century when they conquered Sicily, and the Italians took the dried pasta idea and ran with it, making their pasta out of hard durum wheat and cutting the noodles by hand. By the early 12th century, Sicily had the first known pasta factory and was a major exporter of spaghetti. Early versions of the extrusion press appeared in the 14th century and allowed pasta makers to experiment with different shapes of pasta, but the machines weren't well established until the Renaissance, when technological advances allowed pasta to be mass produced on an unprecedented scale.

Although people were no doubt dressing their pasta with sauce throughout Italy since the Middle Ages, there are very few records of the sauces they used. Cookbooks were written for the wealthy, not the lower classes, so the sauces of the home cooks are not well documented. There is much regional variation in Italy, and recipes differ greatly depending on where they were prepared. After the unification of Italy, Pelligrino Artusi, often called the Father of Italian Cuisine, gathered recipes from all over the country, highlighting and celebrating the regional differences. With his cookbook, which was published in 1891, he was trying to pull the country together with a national cuisine. From his work and a spattering of other cookbooks from the 18th and 19th centuries, we gather that tomato sauces for pasta were used by the late 18th century, at least among the lower classes, while meat-based sauces predominated among the upper class. By the time Artusi compiled the recipes for his cookbook, tomato sauces were widespread throughout Italy in all social classes.

Marinara

Marinara Sauce is probably the best known of Italy's two reigning tomato sauces (the other being Pomodoro Sauce). When you picture a plate of pasta with a chunky tomato sauce, you are thinking of Marinara Sauce. Although most people think of tomato sauce as inherently Italian, it has only been part of Italian cuisine since the late 17th century. Tomatoes, which were introduced to Europe by Spanish sailors returning to their homeland from colonies in Mesoamerica, were slow to catch on in Italy. Tomato sauces were well established in Spain long before they appeared in Italy, though they were served over meat, not pasta. In Italy, tomato sauce first appeared in Naples when the city was still owned by Spain, where it was known as Spanish-style Sauce (*alla Spagnuola*) and was served over meat and fish. It is unclear when tomato sauce began to be served over pasta, but the pairing appears in an Italian cookbook as early as 1790.

Olive oil	2/3 cup	150 mL
Finely chopped onion	1 cup	250 mL
Finely chopped carrot	3/4 cup	175 mL
Finely chopped celery	3/4 cup	175 mL
Can of whole tomatoes (28 oz., 796 mL), with juice	1	1
Garlic cloves, minced	3	3
Italian seasoning	1 tbsp.	15 mL
Granulated sugar	2 tsp.	10 mL
Bay leaf	1	1
Salt	1 tsp.	5 mL
Pepper	1/2 tsp.	2 mL

Heat olive oil in a large pot on medium. Add next 3 ingredients and cook, stirring occasionally, for about 10 minutes until onions are softened.

Stir in remaining 7 ingredients. Reduce heat to medium-low and simmer, uncovered, for about 30 minutes, stirring occasionally, until slightly thickened. Remove bay leaf. Remove pot from heat and process briefly with an immersion blender. The sauce is not meant to be smooth. Store in an airtight container in refrigerator for 5 to 7 days, or freeze. Makes 6 cups (1.5 L)

Bolognese

As its name suggests, this popular sauce hails from Bologna, the capital of the Emilia-Romagna region of northern Italy, where it is known as Ragu alla Bolognese or simply Ragu. This meaty sauce dates back at least to 1891, when it appeared in Pelligrino Artusi's famed Italian cookbook, *La Scienza in Cucina e L'arte di Mangiar Bene* (The Science of Cooking and the Art of Eating Well). Artusi, often called The Father of Italian Cuisine, included finely minced pancetta and veal fillets instead of the bacon and ground beef more commonly seen today. Ragu purists insist that authentic Bolognese Sauce should contain no tomato and be served over tagliatelle, a flat, ribbon-shaped pasta that originated in the Emilia-Romagna region, or nestled between lasagna noodles in Lasagne alla Bolognese. However, today there are many variations of Bolognese, both with or without tomato, and they are equally delicious served over any pasta that is sturdy enough to handle this thick sauce.

Bacon slices, chopped	4	4
Lean ground beef	1 lb.	454 g
Finely chopped carrot	1/2 cup	125 mL
Finely chopped celery	1/2 cup	125 mL
Finely chopped onion	1/2 cup	125 mL
Garlic cloves, minced (or 1/2 tsp., 2 mL, powder)	2	2
Salt	1/2 tsp.	2 mL
Pepper	1/4 tsp.	1 mL
Tomato paste (see Tip, page 82)	1/3 cup	75 mL
Prepared beef broth	1 cup	250 mL
Dry (or alcohol-free) red wine	1/2 cup	125 mL
Half-and-half cream	1/4 cup	60 mL

Cook bacon in a large saucepan on medium until crisp. Remove with a slotted spoon to a plate lined with paper towel to drain. Drain and discard all but 1 tsp. (5 mL) drippings.

Add next 7 ingredients to same pot. Scramble-fry for about 10 minutes until beef is no longer pink.

Add tomato paste. Heat, stirring, for 1 minute. Stir in broth, wine and bacon. Bring to a boil. Reduce heat to medium-low. Simmer, covered, for 1 hour to blend flavours.

Stir in cream. Store in an airtight container in refrigerator for 3 to 4 days. Makes 4 cups (1 L).

Puttanesca

This colourful sauce has an equally colourful name: *puttanesca* means "in the manner of a prostitute" in Italian, and the sauce is often referred to as "whore sauce." Food historians offer several theories for how this name came to be. Some suggest that this dish was a favourite of prostitutes who needed to grab a quick meal between clients; others suggest that the name comes from the pungent combination of black olives, capers and anchovies, which may have a scent reminiscent of a "lady of the night." Yet another theory proposes that a group of hungry customers descended upon a restaurant at closing time and begged the owner to throw together a quick meal out of whatever he had on hand. This sauce is thought to have originated in Naples, most likely in the mid-20th century.

Olive oil	2 tbsp.	30 mL
Chopped onion	1 cup	250 mL
Garlic cloves, minced	3	3
Dried crushed chilies	1/2 tsp.	2 mL
Can of diced tomatoes (28 oz., 796 mL), with juice	1	1
Sliced Kalamata olives	1/2 cup	125 mL
Flat leaf (Italian) parsley, chopped	1/4 cup	60 mL
Capers	2 tbsp.	30 mL
Red wine vinegar	1 tbsp.	15 mL
Chopped oregano	1 tbsp.	15 mL
Anchovy paste (see Tip, below)	1 tsp.	5 mL
Liquid honey	1 tsp.	5 mL

Heat olive oil in a large pot on medium. Add next 3 ingredients. Cook, stirring often, for about 5 minutes until onion is softened.

Stir in remaining 8 ingredients and bring to a boil. Reduce heat to a simmer and cook, stirring occasionally, for about 15 minutes to allow flavours to combine. Store in an airtight container in refrigerator for 4 to 5 days. Makes 6 servings.

Tip: If you prefer not to use anchovy paste, replace it with 1 tsp. (5 mL) of Worcestershire sauce and 1/2 tsp. (2 mL) of salt.

Arrabiata

The Italian word *arrabiata* translates to "angry" in English. Some suggest Arrabiata Sauce gets its name for the heat the chilies bring to the sauce, assuming that "angry" actually means "spicy." Another theory suggests that the sauce is so named because when you eat it, its spicy flavour will make your face flushed and sweaty, much as it might be if you were angry. The history of this sauce is murky, but it seems to have originated in Rome, perhaps sometime in the early 20th century, and it was immortalized in Italian film director and screenwriter Federico Fellini's 1972 film *Roma*. In this recipe, we have added chopped bacon for a little extra flair. If you prefer a more traditional Arrabiata, leave out the bacon and add 2 tsp. (5 mL) of olive oil. This sauce is traditionally served over penne, but longer noodles, such as spaghetti, also work well. For an authentic Penne Arrabiata, sprinkle a little pecorino cheese overtop before serving.

Bacon slices, chopped	4	4
Can of diced tomatoes (14 oz., 398 mL) with juice	1	1
White wine vinegar	1 tbsp.	15 mL
Garlic clove, minced	1	1
Dried crushed chilies	1/2 tsp.	2 mL
Granulated sugar	1/4 tsp.	1 mL
Salt	1/8 tsp.	0.5 mL
Pepper	1/8 tsp.	0.5 mL
Finely shredded fresh basil	1 tbsp.	15 mL

Cook bacon in a large frying pan on medium until crisp. Transfer with a slotted spoon to a plate lined with paper to drain. Drain and discard all but 2 tsp. (10 mL) drippings.

Add next 7 ingredients to same frying pan. Cook for 5 minutes, stirring occasionally. Stir in bacon and cook, stirring, for about 2 minutes to blend flavours.

Sprinkle with basil. Store in an airtight container in refrigerator for 4 to 5 days, or freeze. Makes about 1 1/2 cups (375 mL).

Vodka Sauce

Even though it is a relatively new sauce (at least when compared to traditional French sauces) the origins of Vodka Sauce are disputed. Some claim that it originated in Italy in the 1970s, whereas others believe that it was created in the United States by an Italian chef in either the 1970s or '80s. One of the most popular origin stories claims that the sauce was created by a chef who was paid by a vodka company to promote their product. Another story suggests that an Italian chef needed to thin out the sauce he was cooking and had only vodka on hand. Regardless of its origins, this rich, creamy sauce pairs especially well with pasta and is an integral part of the popular dish Penne alla Vodka.

Olive oil	2 tbsp.	30 mL
Butter	1 tbsp.	15 mL
Finely chopped onion	1 1/4 cups	300 mL
Garlic cloves, minced	2	2
Finely chopped oregano	1 tbsp.	15 mL
Dried crushed chilies	1/4 tsp.	60 mL
Vodka	1/2 cup	125 mL
Can of crushed tomatoes (28 oz., 796 mL)	1	1
Salt	1/2 tsp.	2 mL
Pepper	1/2 tsp.	2 mL
Whipping cream	1/2 cup	125 mL
Chopped oregano	2 tbsp.	30 mL

Heat olive oil and butter in a large pot on medium. Add onions and cook, stirring often, until soft, about 5 minutes.

Add garlic, oregano and dried crush chilies. Cook, stirring often, until fragrant, about 2 minutes.

Stir in vodka and simmer until reduced by about half, about 3 to 5 minutes.

Stir in tomatoes, salt and pepper, and bring to a simmer. Decrease heat to medium-low and cook, covered, for 35 to 40 minutes to allow flavours to blend.

Stir in cream. Bring sauce to a simmer, stirring occasionally. Remove from heat. Stir in second amount of oregano. Store in an airtight container in refrigerator for 5 to 7 days. Makes 4 cups (1 L).

Alfredo

Made famous as the sauce component of Fettuccini Alfredo, this sauce was named for Alfredo di Lelio, a restauranteur from Rome, Italy. In the early 1900s, di Lelio served his queasy pregnant wife a simple dish of pasta tossed with butter and Parmesan cheese, a common way of dressing pasta as far back as the Middle Ages until at least the mid-1800s. She enjoyed it so much that he added it to his menu. In 1920, two famous American actors—Mary Pickford and Douglas Fairbanks—visited di Lelio's restaurant and loved the dish. They brought the recipe back home with them but without access to the rich Italian butter and Parmesan cheese di Lelio used in his dish (Parmesan cheese was not readily available in the U.S. until well after World War II), the flavour was not the same. American chefs made a variety of adjustments, most notably the addition of cream and sometimes garlic, to try to emulate the flavour of di Lelio's dish, resulting in the sauce we know today.

Butter	1/4 cup	60 mL
Garlic cloves, minced	2	2
Whipping cream	1 cup	250 mL
Grated Parmesan cheese	1/2 cup	125 mL
Salt	1/4 tsp.	1 mL
Coarsely ground pepper	1/4 tsp.	1 mL

Melt butter in a small saucepan on medium heat. Add garlic and cook, stirring, for about 1 minute until fragrant.

Stir in whipping cream. Bring to a boil on medium heat. Boil gently, uncovered, for about 3 or 4 minutes, stirring occasionally, until slightly reduced and thickened. Remove from heat.

Add next 3 ingredients, stirring until cheese is melted. Store in an airtight container in refrigerator for up to 3 days. Makes 2 cups (500 mL).

Classic Pesto

Also known as Pesto Genovese, this classic herb sauce originated in Genoa, in the Liguria region of Italy. The name "pesto" comes from the Italian word *pestere*, which means "to pound" or "grind," and the sauce was so named because it was traditionally made by grinding the ingredients with a mortar and pestle. Pesto purists would argue that for the best flavour it should still be made that way, but the blender does a great job with less effort. Sauces made of ingredients ground together by mortar and pestle date back to at least the ancient Romans, though they wouldn't have contained the basil that gives pesto its distinctive flavour. Liguria is famous for its basil, which is thought to be milder and sweeter than basil grown elsewhere in Italy and has been a staple in the region since Medieval times. Genoa has long been a trading port, and sailors leaving from there took pesto around the world with them in their travels. There are myriad variations of pesto today, with different regions adding their own touches, but the traditional version contained only basil, garlic, pine nuts, olive oil and Parmesan cheese.

Fresh basil leaves, packed	2 cups	500 mL
Olive oil	1/4 cup	60 mL
Pine nuts, toasted (see Tip, page 128)	1/4 cup	60 mL
Garlic cloves	3	3
Salt	1/4 tsp.	1 mL
Grated Parmesan cheese	1/2 cup	125 mL

Process first 5 ingredients in a blender or food processor until smooth. Transfer to a small bowl.

Stir in cheese. Store in an airtight container in refrigerator for up to 3 days. To keep pesto from drying out, lay a piece of plastic wrap over surface of pesto before covering with lid or store in freezer. Makes about 1 cup (250 mL).

Gremolata

Traditionally, this simple, flavourful sauce has only three ingredients: parsley, lemon zest and garlic. It is an essential part of Osso Bucco alla Milanese, an iconic braised veal shank dish from Milan that is smothered with gremolata and served on a bed of risotto. This versatile sauce is also amazing on steak, chicken, lamb and green vegetables, such as green beans and asparagus, and it can be stirred into soups and stews or added to pasta or rice for a delicious flavour boost. We've added pine nuts and Parmesan cheese to this recipe to give the sauce some depth and crunch, but if you prefer the classic version, you can leave them out without skimping on flavour. The key to this sauce is to use the freshest ingredients possible.

Minced Italian parsley	1/2 cup	125 mL
Grated Parmesan cheese	1/4 cup	60 mL
Pine nuts, toasted (see Tip, page 128)	1/4 cup	60 mL
Garlic cloves, minced	5	5
Lemon zest (see Tip, page 108)	2 1/2 tbsp.	37 mL

Combine all 5 ingredients in a medium bowl. Best served same day but can be stored in an airtight container in refrigerator for to 2 to 3 days. Makes about 1 cup (250 mL).

Classic Pesto

Italian Salsa Verde

Simple green parsley-based sauces were popular throughout much of Europe as far back as Medieval times. The origins of Italian Salsa Verde are unknown, but Pelligrino Artusi included a similar version with the same name in his famous 1891 Italian cookbook, *La Scienza in Cucina e L'arte di Mangiar Bene.* In his book, Artusi collected recipes from all over the different regions of a recently unified Italy with the intention of creating a national culinary identity. As with many sauces that have a long history, Italian Salsa Verde has many variations, with every region adding their own special touches. The result is a wonderfully versatile sauce that is usually served with beef, poultry or fish.

Fresh Italian parsley	3/4 cup	175 mL
Fresh basil	3/4 cup	175 mL
Fresh mint	1/4 cup	60 mL
Chives	1/4 cup	60 mL
Garlic cloves	3	3
Anchovy fillets	2	2
Capers	2 tbsp.	30 mL
Dried crushed chilies	1 tsp.	5 mL
Lemon zest (see Tip, page 108)	1/2 tsp.	2 mL
Olive oil	2/3 cup	150 mL
Lemon juice	2 tbsp.	30 mL
White wine vinegar	1 tbsp.	15 mL
Salt	1/4 tsp.	1 mL
Pepper	1/4 tsp.	1 mL

Pulse first 9 ingredients in a food processor until herbs are coarsely chopped.

Add remaining 5 ingredients and pulse until well combined. Store in an airtight container in refrigerator for up to 3 days. Makes 1 1/2 cups (375 mL).

Salmoriglio

This sauce, which can also be used as a marinade or dipping sauce, hails from Sicily. The name *salmoriglio* means "little brine," referring to the sauce's salty flavour. Salt was a coveted commodity in the ancient world, important both for preserving and seasoning food. It was as valuable as gold, and in ancient Rome, was even used as currency (Roman soldiers were paid in salt for their service). Sicily has a long history of salt production, possibly dating back to the Phoenicians, who settled in the area around 800 BCE. By the late Middle Ages, lagoons along Sicily's west coast were prolific "salt factories" supplying the Mediterranean and eventually much of Europe. Sicilian salt is said to have a unique flavour that pairs especially well with fish (fishing being another industry that has been important in the country since ancient times), so it is no wonder that this sauce is usually served with grilled fish.

Fresh oregano, minced	1/2 cup	125 mL
Garlic cloves, minced	3	3
Lemon juice	3 tbsp.	45 mL
Lemon zest (see Tip, below)	2 tsp.	10 mL
Olive oil	3/4 cup	175 mL
Hot water	1/4 cup	60 mL
Salt	1/2 tsp.	2 mL
Pepper	1/4 tsp.	1 mL

Combine first 4 ingredients in a medium bowl.

Combine oil and water in a separate bowl. Add in a slow stream to garlic mixture , whisking until emulsified.

Season with salt and pepper. Store in an airtight container in refrigerator for up to 5 days. Makes about 1 cup (250 mL).

Tip: When a recipe calls for grated zest and juice, it's easier to grate the fruit first, then juice it. Be careful not to grate down to the pith (the white part of the peel), which is bitter and is best avoided.

Bagna Cauda

One of the lesser-known Italian sauces, Bagna Cauda originated in the Piedmont region of northwestern Italy, where it is often served at Christmas or New Years, as well as at the end of the grape harvest. The name translates to "hot bath," most likely in reference to the way this sauce is served. It is a dipping sauce meant for sharing, traditionally served fondue-style in individual terracotta warming pots called *fojot,* with vegetable crudités or bread for dipping. Although the specific origins of the sauce are unclear, some food historians have suggested that it likely has roots in the fish sauces that were popular in ancient Greece and Rome.

Extra virgin olive oil	3/4 cup	175 mL
Unsalted butter, softened	1/3 cup	75 mL
Anchovy fillets	12	12
Garlic cloves, sliced	8	8

Salt, to taste
Pepper, to taste

Combine all 4 ingredients in a food processor until smooth. Transfer mixture to a small saucepan. Cook over low heat for about 13 to 15 minutes, stirring occasionally, to allow flavours to blend.

Season with salt and pepper. Transfer to a small fondue pot and keep warm. This sauce does not store or reheat well. Makes about 1 cup (250 mL).

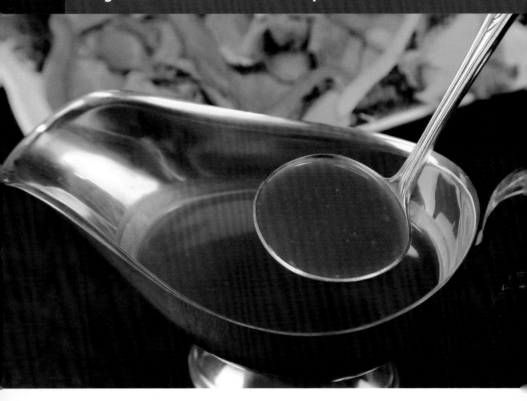

English Cuisine: A Historical Perspective

From the Romans and the Anglo-Saxons to the Vikings and the French, England has had a long history of domination, and each culture has influenced British culture and cuisine. Wine, grapes, cherries, plums, olive oil, garlic, rabbits, pheasants and black pepper and are only some of the foods the Romans are credited with introducing to England (not to mention an expansive road system to move the food about). Britain's history as a trading partner and colonial power have also left their mark. Take, for example, tea from China, sugar from the Caribbean and curry from India, to name a few. A look at England's cuisine provides a fascinating window into the country's history.

In Medieval times, sauces in England were thickened with bread crumbs (much like they were in ancient Rome). A modern-day sauce still made in this way is bread sauce, a popular addition to the traditional Christmas dinner. Served over roast turkey or chicken, bread sauce at its most basic is made of milk thickened with stale bread crumbs. Sometimes meat drippings or aromatics like onion are added, and it is often seasoned with mace, pepper, cloves, bay leaves and salt, all of which were also popular Medieval spices.

The use of drippings from cooking meat as a sauce goes back to antiquity, and in Medieval times a sauce known as *gravé* was a dipping sauce, rather like what we know today as *au jus*. A gravy thickened with flour, as is common today, seems to be an English innovation dating to the mid-1800s, using the French technique of a roux. Gravy is still hugely popular in England and is an essential part of such British classics as the Sunday roast dinner with Yorkshire pudding, and bangers and mash.

The Full English Breakfast dates back to the feasts of Medieval times, where the wealthy showed off their status through the quality, quantity and variety of food they served. Breakfasts feasts were often served before a hunt or a long voyage, or after a night of revelry. By Victorian times, the English breakfast had become an important social event. The Victorians took great pleasure in trying to outdo each other by serving the most exotic or impressive ingredients they could find. By the early 1900s, the meal had become standard fare for the lower classes as well as the upper crust, and it included the ingredients we know today: bacon, sausages, eggs, baked beans, tomatoes, mushrooms, toast, sometimes black pudding and of course, the ubiquitous Brown Sauce.

The national dish of England, fish and chips has its roots in mainland Europe, not Britain. Although the pairing of fish and deep fried poatoes as a dish seems to have originated in London in the 1800s, both the fried fish and the chips arrived in England much earlier. Jewish refugees from Spain and Portugal settled in London in the 1600s, bringing their fish-cooking techniques with them. French fries actually originated in Belgium in the late 1680s and were well established in London by the mid-1800s. The Tartar Sauce served alongside the fish and chips is French in origin.

Clearly the English have adopted many foods and culinary techniques from other cultures and made them their own.

Cumberland

This sauce follows in the tradition of the sweet/sour/spicy fruit sauces that date back to at least Medieval times. The early fruit sauces would have been soured with verjuice, a highly acidic juice made of sour fruit, especially unripe grapes or crab apples. Cumberland Sauce, which is thought to date back around the mid-1800s, uses lemon juice instead. The exact origins of this sauce are a matter of debate. Some claim that it is of German origin, created in Hanover and named for the Duke of Cumberland, who was crown prince of Hanover before his family was exiled after the Austro-Prussian War. Others claim that the sauce originated in England and is named for the Cumberland region, a historic area in northwest England that is now part of Cumbria. Whatever its origin, this sauce is classically served with dark meat such as duck, venison and other wild game. It is best served at room temperature or cold.

Orange	1	1
Lemon	1	1
Red currant jelly	3/4 cup	175 mL
Port wine	1/2 cup	125 mL
Dijon mustard	1 tbsp.	15 mL
Dry ginger	1/2 tsp.	125 mL
Salt	1/4 tsp.	1 mL
Ground cayenne pepper	1/8 tsp.	0.5 mL

Zest lemon and orange, removing only coloured part of peel, not white part (pith) underneath (see Tip, page 108). Set orange and lemon aside. Cut peel into thin strips and transfer to a small saucepan. Add enough water to cover and bring to a boil. Reduce heat to a simmer and cook for about 7 minutes. Drain and set aside.Squeeze juice from orange and lemon to make about 1/2 cup (125 mL) combined, adding extra juice or water if necessary.

Heat jelly in a medium saucepan on medium until melted.

Stir in next 5 ingredients until well incorporated. Stir in orange and lemon juice and bring to a boil. Reduce heat to a simmer and cook for about 10 minutes, stirring occasionally until reduced by a quarter. Remove from heat and stir in blanched peels. Let cool before serving. Store remaining sauce in an airtight container in refrigerator for up to 7 days. Makes about 1 1/2 cups (375 mL).

Brown Sauce

One of the most popular sauces in Britain, Brown Sauce is essentially a fruitier, anchovy-free version of Worcestershire Sauce that gets its flavour from tomato, tamarind paste, vinegar and spices. Although this beloved sauce is traditionally served with the English full breakfast, which includes eggs, sausage, bacon, beans, tomatoes, mushrooms and sometimes black pudding, it is incredibly versatile and is used to flavour many other dishes. There is a sentiment in England that the only British food you can't add Brown Sauce to is tea. Although there are a number of smaller, regional brands, the most popular commercially prepared Brown Sauce in Britain is HP sauce, which was created by a grocer named Frederick Gibson Garton around 1895. He named it HP sauce for the House of Parliament after he heard that it was popular there.

Chopped apple	3 cups	750 mL
Chopped plum	3 cups	750 mL
Chopped onion	3/4 cups	175 mL
Garlic cloves, minced	8	8
Malt vinegar	2 cups	500 mL
Brown sugar	1/2 cup	125 mL
Kosher salt	1 tbsp.	15 mL
Tamarind paste (see page 132)	1 tbsp.	15 mL
Tomato paste (see Tip, page 82)	1 tbsp.	15 mL
Ground ginger	1/2 tsp.	2 mL
Ground allspice	1/2 tsp.	2 mL
Ground nutmeg	1/2 tsp.	2 mL
Ground cayenne pepper	1/4 tsp.	1 mL

Combine first 7 ingredients in a large saucepan on medium-low heat. Cook, stirring occasionally, until soft, about 25 to 30 minutes. Carefully process with an immersion blender or in a blender until smooth, following manufacturer's safety instructions for processing hot liquids.

Stir in next 6 ingredients and bring to a boil. Reduce to a simmer and cook, stirring occasionally, until sauce is reduced and thickened to your desired consistency, about 45 to 60 minutes. Store in an airtight container in refrigerator for up to 5 days. Makes 3 cups (750 mL).

Mint Sauce

Mint is believed to have been used in sauces at least as early as ancient Roman times, and the Romans are sometimes credited with bringing mint sauce to Britain, where it is now customarily served with roast lamb. According to food lore, the pairing of mint sauce with lamb came about in Elizabethan times, when Queen Elizabeth passed a decree that lamb and mutton had to be served with bitter herbs. The decree was meant to bolster the wool industry by discouraging people from eating lamb; however, people soon realized that mint sauce enhanced the flavour of the meat, and a tradition was born.

Finely chopped mint leaves	1/2 cup	125 mL
Boiling water	1/2 cup	125 mL
White wine vinegar	1/4 cup	60 mL
Granulated sugar	3 tbsp.	45 mL
Salt	1/2 tsp.	2 mL
Coarsely ground pepper	1/4 tsp.	1 mL

Combine all 6 ingredients in a medium heat-proof bowl, stirring until sugar has dissolved. Cover bowl and set aside to steep for about 40 to 45 minutes, allowing mint flavours to infuse into vinegar and sugar. If sauce is too strong, add more water; if it is too weak, add more mint. Store in a jar or airtight container in refrigerator for up to 7 days. Makes about 1 cup (250 mL).

South and Southeast Asian Cuisine: A Historical Perspective

The countries of modern-day Southeast Asia have been shaped by a long history of trade and occupation. Trade routes between India, southeast Asia, the Middle East and China were well established by the first century BCE, long before the Europeans came on the scene. Tradeable goods were not the only things that passed along these routes; cultural knowledge, ideas and traditions also flowed between the peoples in these countries. As such, the disparate cultures in these regions intermingled, influencing each other. The cultural exchange is evident in the culinary traditions in Southeast Asia; although the different countries have their own unique culinary styles, they also have many similarities.

Southeast Asia can be divided into mainland and island countries. The mainland countries, Cambodia, Laos, Myanmar, Vietnam, Thailand and Singapore, are nestled between India and China, two historically dominant trading powers that had established overland trade routes in antiquity. Mainland Southeast Asia has a long coastline, and the peoples in these regions took advantage of the maritime trading routes between the two superpowers. The prevailing winds in the area also made the islands of Southeast Asia important meeting points for trade between India and China. It is no surprise, then, that these two nations have had a great deal of influence on the culture of the region.

India exported textiles to the Spice Islands and Southeast Asia, including the Malay peninsula and Thailand. They also traded in cotton, indigo, sugar and rice. As India expanded their trade routes across the Bay of Bengal, so too, did they strengthen their influence on the peoples they traded with.

Indian influences are strong and easily evident in the culinary traditions of Laos, Cambodia, northern Vietnam, Thailand, Java, Myanmar and Bali, where curries have been widely adopted.

For the islands of Southeast Asia, it is often said that "the land divides, and the sea unites." Because the interior of the islands was often covered with lush, impenetrable jungle or difficult terrain, it was easier for people along the coasts to travel by boat to nearby islands than it was to travel across the islands. The result was that people traded more and were more closely connected with the people on neighbouring islands than they were with those in the interior or on opposite side of their own island. These connections created pockets of shared language and culture that are not reflected in modern political boundaries. For example, Singapore, Indonesia and Malaysia, today separate political entities, share the same language, history of trade and style of cooking, even though each has put their own spin on cooking methods and use of ingredients.

China has also had an enormous influence on Southeast Asia. In antiquity, tribal groups from China moved along the river systems into Southeast Asia, eventually leading to the colonization of Vietnam, where China ruled for 10 centuries from around 100 to 1000 CE. Not only did the Chinese introduce Confucianism, Taoism and Buddhism to Vietnam, they also influenced the local cuisine. Ingredients such as soy sauce, tofu, noodles and wontons were introduced by the Chinese, as were the use of chopsticks, stir-frying and deep-frying food in a wok.

In slightly more modern times, the spice trade also had an impact on the cultures of Southeast Asia. The Spice Islands (Malaku, or the Moluccas), northeast of Indonesia, generated a worldwide trade network dating back to Roman and Greek times, but things got messy once the Europeans decided to skip the middlemen in the trading system and go directly to the source. As a result, the Dutch ruled Indonesia for almost 400 years, no doubt leaving a lasting impression. The French and British established colonies in India. France also colonized Vietnam, and their influence can be seen in the Vietnamese appreciation of coffee and bread (in the form of baguettes, which are still popular today, though they are made with rice flour, not wheat flour), foods that do not feature heavily in other Southeast Asian countries. The Portuguese introduced the chili pepper from Mesoamerica, and it was widely adopted in the cuisines of the region. Arabic influences in the area are evident in Indonesia and Malaysia, where pork barely features on the menu.

Although outside influences have left their mark, there are many similarities in the local culinary traditions of the peoples of Southeast Asia. The artificial modern-day political boundaries imposed on the region do not reflect the diverse yet connected cultures of the area, as is evident in their distinct yet still fundamentally similar cuisines.

Curry Sauce

There is no one true curry sauce. In fact, there are probably more than a hundred. Curry is a catch-all name for the many anglicized versions of authentic Indian dishes. When the British East India Company ruled India for much of the 17th and 18th centuries, many British soldiers (and sometimes their families) were stationed there. These British expats found the flavours of Indian cuisine a little too strong for their liking, so they refashioned the dishes to suit their palate. The word "curry" is thought to be a mispronunciation of *kari* or *karil*, which were historically local terms for spicy dishes of sauteed vegetables or meat but now simply mean "sauce" or "gravy." In truth, the people of India do not use the word "curry"; their curries have specific names and differ from region to region.

Vegetable oil	2 tbsp.	30 mL
Ghee	2 tbsp.	30 mL
Medium onion, finely chopped	1	1
Garlic cloves, minced	6	6
Minced ginger root	2 tbsp.	30 mL
Curry powder	2 tbsp.	30 mL
Ground cumin	1 tsp.	5 mL
Ground coriander	1 tsp.	5 mL
Paprika	1/2 tsp.	2 mL
Prepared chicken broth	3 1/2 cups	875 mL
Whipping cream	1 cup	250 mL
Cornstarch	1 tbsp.	15 mL
Brown sugar, packed	2 tsp.	10 mL
Salt, to taste		
Pepper, to taste		

Heat oil and ghee in a large saucepan on medium heat. Add onion and cook until softened but not browned, about 6 minutes.

Stir in next 6 ingredients and cook until fragrant, about 1 minute.

Stir in broth. Bring to a simmer and cook, stirring frequently, for about 20 to 25 minutes until it has reduced to about 3 cups (750 mL).

Whisk next 3 ingredients in a medium bowl until cornstarch and brown sugar are dissolved. Whisk cornstarch mixture into Curry Sauce. Return sauce to a simmer, stirring occasionally, until sauce is thickened. Season to taste with salt and pepper. Store in an airtight container in refrigerator for 3 to 4 days. Makes about 4 cups (1 L).

Vindaloo Sauce

Although this spicy sauce is among one of India's best-known dishes, its origins are in fact Portuguese. Before the Portuguese arrived in India in the 15th century, the hottest spice in the region was black pepper. The chilies that flavour much of the food today were introduced to the Goa region by Portuguese sailors who brought them from the Portuguese colony in Brazil. The sailors also brought with them dish that Vindaloo Sauce was based on. Locals adapted the Portuguese recipe using locally available ingredients and spices, transforming the original dish into the sauce we are familiar with today. Vindaloo is most popular with pork and chicken but it pairs well with potatoes too.

Cooking oil	2 tbsp.	30 mL
Chopped onion	1 1/2 cups	375 mL
Garlic cloves, minced	5	5
Jalapeño or serrano pepper, seeded, and chopped fine (see Tip, page 160)	1 tbsp.	15 mL
Ground cumin	2 tsp.	10 mL
Turmeric	1 tsp.	5 mL
Minced ginger root	1 tsp.	5 mL
Paprika	1/2 tsp.	2 mL
Ground coriander	1/2 tsp.	2 mL
Ground cayenne pepper	1/2 tsp.	2 mL
Salt	1/2 tsp.	2 mL
Pepper	1/4 tsp.	1 mL
Prepared chicken broth	1 1/2 cups	375 mL
Can of diced tomatoes (14 oz., 398 mL), with juice	1	1
Red wine vinegar	2 tbsp.	30 mL

Heat oil in a medium saucepan on medium. Add onion and cook until softened and slightly brown, about 7 minutes.

Add next 10 ingredients and cook, stirring constantly, until fragrant, about 2 minutes.

Stir in chicken broth, scraping any brown bits from bottom of pan.

Stir in tomatoes and vinegar and bring to a simmer. Cook, stirring occasionally, until sauce has reduced to about 4 cups (1 L), about 15 minutes. Carefully process with an immersion blender or in a blender until smooth, following manufacturer's safety instructions for processing hot liquids. Store in an airtight container in refrigerator for 5 to 7 days. Makes about 4 cups (1 L).

Tikka Masala

The origins of this widely popular sauce are hotly disputed. Some people claim that it was created in the 1970s in Glasgow, Scotland, by a chef trying to appease a customer who sent his chicken curry back because it was too dry. The chef added a little tomato soup to the dish, and Tikka Masala Sauce was born. Other people maintain that Tikka Masala originated in the Indian subcontinent, perhaps in what is today Bangladesh. Whatever the origin, there is no doubt that the sauce is quintessentially Indian in nature, using traditional ingredients and techniques from Indian cuisine. Though it is commonly served with chicken, it can be paired with your protein of choice and served over plain white rice.

Cooking oil	1 tbsp.	15 mL
Ghee	1 tbsp.	15 mL
Chopped onion	1 cup	250 mL
Garlic cloves, minced	2	2
Minced ginger root	2 tsp.	10 mL
Garam masala	2 tsp.	10 mL
Turmeric	1 tsp.	5 mL
Salt	1 tsp.	5 mL
Paprika	1/2 tsp.	2 mL
Ground cayenne pepper	1/2 tsp.	2 mL
Can of diced tomatoes (14 oz., 398 mL), with juice	1	1
Tomato sauce	1 cup	250 mL
Whipping cream	1/2 cup	125 mL
Chopped cilantro	1/4 cup	60 mL

Heat oil and ghee in a medium saucepan on medium. Add onion and cook for 5 to 6 minutes until beginning to soften.

Stir in next 7 ingredients. Cook, stirring constantly, for about 2 minutes until fragrant.

Turn heat to medium-low. Stir in diced tomatoes and tomato sauce until well combined. Bring to a simmer and cook for about 10 minutes, until flavours are combined and sauce has reduced by a quarter.

Whisk in cream and simmer for 10 minutes, whisking occasionally.

Garnish with fresh cilantro. Store in an airtight container in refrigerator for 5 to 7 days. Makes about 3 1/2 cups (875 mL).

Cilantro Sauce

Cilantro has a long history of culinary use and in ancient times was even used medicinally. It features heavily in Asian cuisine, even though it is not native to the region. Cilantro is native to the Mediterranean region and is thought to have spread to Asia and Africa via ancient trade routes. The Romans are credited with introducing cilantro to Britain, and likely to their provinces in western Asia as well, and indirectly to southeast Asia using middlemen (possibly the Persians). This sauce pairs well with grilled foods including meats, tofu or cauliflower, as well as steamed vegetable and rice.

Cilantro	2 cups	500 mL
Mint leaves	1/3 cup	75 mL
Chopped cashew nuts, toasted (see Tip, below)	1/4 cup	60 mL
Garlic cloves, minced	3	3
Lime juice	1 tbsp.	15 mL
Fish sauce	1 tbsp.	15 mL
Grated gingerroot	1 tsp.	5 mL
Red Thai chili, chopped and seeded (see Tip, page 160)	1/2 tsp.	2 mL
Olive oil	1/4 cup	60 mL
Salt, to taste		
Pepper, to taste		

Process first 8 ingredients in a blender or food processor until smooth.

Drizzle in oil until mixture has a creamy and slightly grainy texture. Add extra oil if needed for desired texture. Season with salt and pepper. Store in an airtight container in refrigerator for up to 5 days. Makes about 1 cup (250 mL).

Tip: When toasting nuts, seeds or coconut, cooking times will vary for each type of nut—so never toast them together. For small amounts, place the ingredient in an ungreased shallow frying pan. Heat on medium for 3 to 5 minutes, stirring often, until golden. For larger amounts, spread the ingredient evenly in an ungreased shallow pan. Bake in a 350°F (175°C) oven for 5 to 10 minutes, stirring or shaking often, until golden.

Thai Peanut Sauce

Although peanuts are native to the Americas, most likely South America, peanut sauce is widely popular throughout much of southeast Asia, including the Malay Peninsula and Indonesia. Peanuts made their way into southeast Asia through the Philippines, where they were introduced by Spanish sailors in the 16th century, when the Philippines were part of the Spanish Empire. From there they most likely spread to Indonesia and eventually made their way into the cuisine of much of southeast Asia. Many variations of peanut sauce, also often called Satay Sauce, exist as different regions put their own spin on it, but one ingredient they all have in common is ground roasted peanuts. Serve this Thai Peanut Sauce with any skewer or as a dipping sauce for cooked vegetables.

Fresh cilantro stems, chopped	2 tbsp.	30 mL
Garlic cloves, crushed	2	2
Sambal oelek (chili paste)	1 1/2 tsp.	7 mL
Fish sauce	1 tsp.	5 mL
Sesame oil	1 tsp.	5 mL
Smooth peanut butter	1/2 cup	125 mL
Golden brown sugar, packed	3 tbsp.	45 mL
Rice vinegar	2 tbsp.	30 mL
Coconut milk	1/2 cup	125 mL
Lime juice	3 tbsp.	45 mL
Chopped unsalted peanuts, toasted (see Tip, page 128)	2 tbsp.	30 mL
Finely chopped cilantro	1 tbsp.	15 mL

Grind first 4 ingredients together using a mortar and pestle or coffee grinder until mixture becomes a paste-like consistency.

Heat sesame oil in a small saucepan on medium until hot. Stir in paste and cook until just fragrant, about 2 minutes.

Stir in next 5 ingredients. Heat, stirring constantly, on medium until mixture starts to bubble. Remove from heat and set aside to cool to room temperature.

Stir in peanuts and sprinkle with cilantro. Store in an airtight container in refrigerator for up to 7 days. Makes about 1 1/4 cup (300 mL).

Authentic peanut sauces do not use peanut butter, an American invention, and peanut sauce purists would be horrified at the thought, insisting that ground peanuts bring a lightness and better flavour to the sauce.

Tamarind Sauce

Although originally from Africa, tamarind fruit has become a staple in Asian cuisine, giving dishes a sour-sweet or tangy flavour. Originally brought to India by Arabic traders from Africa, tamarind is now grown widely throughout tropical regions of Asia, central America and the Caribbean. Today Thailand is one of the world's largest producers of the fruit. Tamarind Sauce is incredibly versatile, pairing well with chicken, fish, vegetables and tofu. You can also use it as a dipping sauce with something as simple as onion rings.

Tamarind pulp (see below)	2/3 cup	150 mL
Water	2 cups	500 mL
Granulated sugar	3 tbsp.	45 mL
Garlic cloves, minced	4	4
Sambal oelek (chili paste)	1 tbsp.	15 mL
Ginger root, peeled and grated	1 tbsp.	15 mL
Fish sauce	2 tsp.	10 mL
Soy sauce	1 tsp.	5 mL
Water	3 tbsp.	45 mL
Cornstarch	2 tbsp.	30 mL

Combine tamarind pulp and water in a medium saucepan and bring to a boil over high heat. Remove pan from heat and let stand until tamarind has softened, about 15 minutes. Stir to break up pulp. Press through a fine sieve to extract as much water as possible and discard solids. Return water to pan.

Add next 6 ingredients to saucepan and stir. Bring to a boil over high heat. Reduce the heat and simmer for 5 minutes, stirring frequently.

Combine water and cornstarch, stirring until smooth. Whisk mixture into Tamarind Sauce, continuing to whisk until sauce thickens, about 1 minute. Remove pan from heat and set aside to cool. Before serving, taste and adjust seasoning, adding more sugar if necessary to balance tartness of tamarind. Store Tamarind Sauce in an airtight container in refrigerator for up to 7 days. Makes about 2 1/2 cups (525 mL).

〰 Because fresh tamarind pods are not readily available outside of the tropics, most cooks rely on tamarind pulp or tamarind paste to add to their recipes. Tamarind pulp is sold in a block and still contains the fruit's seeds and fibres. To use it, break a piece off the block, rehydrate it with hot water, then mash it and push it through a fine-mesh sieve. With tamarind paste, all those steps have been done for you, resulting in a paste that can be used straight from the container. Look for the pulp or paste in Indian or Middle Eastern grocery stores.

Thai Green Curry Sauce

This spicy curry sauce is considered one of Thailand's signature dishes. Its Thai name translates to "sweet green curry," but that is not a reference to the flavour of this sauce. "Sweet green" in this case refers to the colour, which comes mostly from the combination of blended Thai green chilies, cilantro and turmeric in the Thai green curry paste. The history of this sauce is unclear, but it seems to be a relatively new sauce, with the first reference to it in print occurring in a cookbook from the early 1900s. This sauce is often served over beef or chicken, though in the southern regions of Thailand it is traditionally served with goat. We prefer to make our own Thai green curry paste, but if you are short on time, there are many premade options on the market.

Fish sauce	2 tbsp.	30 mL
Brown sugar	1 tbsp.	15 mL
Cornstarch	2 tsp.	10 mL
Cooking oil	2 tsp.	10 mL
Tom yum paste	2 tbsp.	30 mL
Garlic cloves, thinly sliced	4	4
Thai green curry paste (see below)	1 tbsp.	15 mL
Turmeric	1/2 tsp.	2 mL
Can of coconut milk (14 oz., 398 mL)	1	1
Prepared chicken broth	1/2 cup	125 mL
Fresh Thai basil leaves	12	12
Lime leaves	4	4

In a small bowl, stir first 3 ingredients until smooth. Set aside.

Heat oil in a small saucepan on medium. Stir in next 4 ingredients and cook until fragrant, about 1 minute.

Add remaining 4 ingredients and bring to a boil. Add fish sauce mixture and whisk constantly until boiling and thickened. Makes about 2 cups (500 mL).

〰 To make Thai green curry paste, add 2 tsp. (10 mL) coriander seeds and 1 tsp. (5 mL) each cumin seed and peppercorns to a small frying pan and cook on medium heat until fragrant, about 1 minute. Set aside to cool. Transfer to a food processor. Add 8 garlic cloves, 2 shallots, 3 Thai green chilies (seeded and chopped), a 5 inch (12.5 cm) long piece of lemon grass (peeled and chopped), 1/3 cup (75 mL) fresh cilantro, 1 tbsp. (15 mL) grated fresh turmeric, 2 tbsp (30 mL) lime juice, 1 tbsp. (15 mL) fish sauce and 1/2 tsp. (2 mL) each ground cinnamon and salt. Process until smooth. Store paste in an airtight container in refrigerator for up to 2 weeks. Makes about 3/4 cup (175 mL).

Nuoc Cham/Vietnamese Chili Dipping Sauce

To make this sauce, the garlic, chilies and sugar would traditionally have been pounded into a thick paste with a mortar and pestle, and then fish sauce, vinegar, lemon juice and water would have been stirred in to reach the desired consistency. Today is it more common to use a blender or food processor to mix the ingredients, but Nuoc Cham Sauce purists swear that the flavour is much better when the sauce is made by hand.

Garlic cloves, chopped	2	2
Fresh small red chilies (seeds and ribs removed for less heat, see Tip, page 160)	3	3
Brown sugar, packed	1 tbsp.	15 mL
Fish sauce	1/4 cup	60 mL
Rice vinegar	3 tbsp.	45 mL
Lime (or lemon) juice	2 tbsp.	30 mL
Water	2 tbsp.	30 mL

Process all 7 ingredients in a blender until garlic and chilies are finely chopped but not puréed. Let stand for at least 10 minutes to blend flavours. Chill for 1 to 2 hours before serving. Store in a jar or airtight container in refrigerator for up to 4 days. Makes 2/3 cup (150 mL).

Spring Roll Dipping Sauce

This is another wonderful dipping sauce for fresh or deep-fried spring rolls. The shredded carrot gives the sauce texture and an extra splash of colour. This sauce is not nearly as spicy as Nuoc Cham but the dried chilies provide a little heat.

Water	1 cup	250 mL
Rice vinegar	3 tbsp.	45 mL
Fish sauce	1/4 cup	60 mL
Finely grated carrot	1 tbsp.	15 mL
Granulated sugar	2 tsp.	10 mL
Garlic clove, crushed	1	1
Dried crushed chilies	1/4 tsp.	1 mL

Combine all 7 ingredients in a small bowl. Let stand for 15 minutes to blend flavours before serving. Store in an airtight container in refrigerator for up to 2 months. Makes 1 1/2 cups (375 mL).

Nuoc Leo/Vietnamese Peanut Sauce

This Vietnamese Peanut Sauce differs from the Thai Peanut Sauce earlier in the book in that it is tomato based instead of using coconut milk. It is also less sweet than the Thai version. This sauce is traditionally served with Vietnamese spring rolls, but is delicious with salad rolls, as well.

Cooking (or chili-flavoured) oil	2 tsp.	10 mL
Garlic cloves, minced	2	2
Sambal oelek (chili paste)	1/2 tsp.	2 mL
Crunchy peanut butter	1/3 cup	75 mL
Can of tomato sauce (7 1/2 oz., 213 mL)	1	1
Brown sugar, packed	2 tsp.	10 mL
Fish sauce	1 tbsp.	15 mL

Heat cooking oil in a small saucepan on medium. Add garlic and cook until soft and golden, about 2 minutes.

Reduce heat to medium-low. Stir in sambal oelek and peanut butter.

Stir in tomato sauce, brown sugar and fish sauce. Simmer for 5 minutes until slightly reduced and thickened. Remove from heat and set aside to cool. Store in a jar or airtight container in refigerator for up to 5 days. Makes about 7/8 cup (200 mL).

East Asian Cuisine: A Historical Perspective

With thousands of years of documented history, China has one of the oldest and most influential civilizations in history. The influence Imperial China had on other cultures in Asia cannot be understated. In east Asia, Korea and Japan adopted many aspects of Chinese culture, including their religion (Buddhism, Taoism and Confucianism), the notion of centralized government, music, architecture and, most importantly in the context of this book, cuisine.

One food common to these three cultures is rice. It is unclear whether rice originated in China or India, but archeological evidence suggests that it was being cultivated in China along the Yangtze River more than 9000 years ago. By the Han Dynasty (around 206 BCE), rice had made its way to southern China. Today China grows almost 30 percent of the world's rice, more than any other country. Rice is not native to Korea and was introduced to the region from southern China somewhere between 1500 and 1000 BCE. It was introduced to Japan from the Korean Peninsula by around 300 BCE. Rice became a staple in all three cultures and is served for almost every meal. It is also ground into flour and used to make noodles, rice cakes and other sweets. Fermented rice is used to make wine: *huangjiu* in China, *cheongju* in Korea and *sake* in Japan. Not only is rice a culinary staple in the three countries, it is also an integral part of each culture, featuring in festivals, folklore and mythology.

Another food staple these countries have in common is soy. Soybeans are native to China and were domesticated by the Zhou Dynasty (1046– 256 BCE). Although people ate both the beans and leaves of the plant, they were not as popular as rice and millet. During the Han Dynasty, the soybean took on a more important role in Chinese cuisine. At this time, Buddhism also came to China, and the religion's precept of non-violence meant that its followers could no longer include meat or fish products in their diet. The traditional fish sauces that dominated Chinese cuisine at the time now needed a plant-based alternative, and a soy-based sauce grew in popularity, eventually eclipsing the fish-based sauces altogether. Soybeans were also used to make soy milk, tofu and other fermented soy products. From China, soybeans spread to Korea and south into Southeast Asia, as well as to Japan. When exactly soybeans arrived in Korea is unknown, but there are records of soy sauce use in Korea by the 7th century, though some historians suggest it was much earlier, around the first century BCE. As for Japan, Buddhist monks are credited with introducing soybeans and other soy products, including soy sauce and tofu, to the island around the 6th century.

These are only two of the many similarities found in the cuisines of East Asia, but other examples abound. Cooking techniques, including stir-frying (the wok dates back to the Han Dynasty in China) and steaming, the use of chopsticks (which also originated in China during the Han Dynasty), the importance of fish and seafood, and the prevalence of fermented foods are shared by all three cultures. In China, archeological evidence suggests that fermenting was already commonplace 9000 years ago. Kimchee, the national dish of Korea, has existed in an early form since about the 3rd century. In Japan, evidence of fermentation dates to the Nara Period (710–794 CE), and fermented foods have shaped the flavour profile of much of the nation's cuisine.

With so much historical trade and empire building in the area, it is unlikely that we will ever unravel how much each culture was influenced by the others, but despite the similarities, each nation has molded its cuisine to suit its own unique character.

Teriyaki

Although we think of it as a sauce, teriyaki is a style of cooking in Japan: it describes a process in which meat or fish is marinated in and then repeatedly brushed with sauce during its cooking time, giving the meat a lustrous shine. Translated to English, *teri* means "shine" and *yaki* means "grilled." This style of cooking dates back to the 1600s in Japan. Teriyaki Sauce, however, is a much more recent invention, and it did not originate in Japan. Food historians have traced its origins back to Hawaii, perhaps as recently as the 1960s, where Japanese settlers created a sweet sauce using soy sauce and locally available pineapple juice.

Soy sauce	3 tbsp.	45 mL
Brown sugar	3 tbsp.	45 mL
Mirin	3 tbsp.	45 mL

Combine all 3 ingredients in a small bowl until smooth. Store in a glass jar or airtight container in refrigerator for up to 3 months. Makes about 1/2 cup (125 mL).

Yakitori

Yakitori is a Japanese term meaning "grilled bird" and usually refers to small pieces of marinated chicken that are skewered and grilled, though other meats prepared in this manner are also sometimes called yakitori, too. It was originally a street food, and the first Yakitori stands appeared in the 1880s. The sauce that dresses the skewers contains many of the usual suspects of Japanese sauces—soy sauce, mirin and sake—but is thicker than most of its contemporaries.

Dark soy sauce	1 cup	250 mL
Sake	1/2 cup	125 mL
Mirin	1/4 tsp.	60 mL
Dark brown sugar	3 tbsp.	45 mL

Combine all ingredients in a small saucepan over medium, stirring until sugar is dissolved. Bring to a boil then reduce heat to a simmer. Cook, stirring occasionally, until sauce has reduced to about half. Remove from heat and set aside to cool. Store in a jar or airtight container in refrigerator for 7 to 8 months. Makes about 1 cup (250 mL).

Teriyaki

Hoisin

Hoisin Sauce is a Chinese dipping sauce, which is also used as a base for many other sauces. It is also known as Peking Sauce and is served with Peking Duck, a dish that is at least 4000 years old. Not much is known about the history of this sauce. The word *hoisin* comes from the Chinese word for "seafood," suggesting either that it was originally served with seafood, or that it may have contained seafood as in ingredient in the past, though modern Hoisin Sauce does not. Today it is sometimes referred to as Chinese barbeque sauce because it is used in much the same way.

Sesame oil	1 1/2 tbsp.	22 mL
Garlic cloves, minced	3	3
Soy sauce	1/2 cup	125 mL
Black bean paste	1/4 cup	60 mL
Dark brown sugar, packed	2 tbsp.	30 mL
Rice wine vinegar	1 1/2 tbsp.	22 mL
Honey	2 tsp.	10 mL
Sambal oelek (chili paste)	1/2 tsp.	2 mL
Pepper	1/4 tsp.	1 mL

Heat oil in a small saucepan over medium. Add garlic and cook until fragrant, about 2 minutes.

Whisk in soy sauce, black bean paste, brown sugar, vinegar, honey and sambal oelek. Cook, whisking occasionally, until sauce has thickened and is smooth. Season with pepper. Set aside to cool. Store in an airtight container in the refrigerator for up to 3 weeks. Makes about 1 cup (250 mL).

For a quicker, uncooked version of this sauce, combine all 9 ingredients in a blender and process until smooth. The sauce will not be quite as flavourful as the cooked version, but it will be smoother.

Ponzu

This sauce is most often served with fish or seafood dishes, particularly as a dipping sauce for firm-fleshed fish that has been sliced very thinly. It is also great over steamed or grilled vegetables. In Japan it is made with *yuzu*, a type of very sour lemon. Although its origins have largely been lost to history, the sauce may have some ties to the Dutch, as the Dutch word *pons* means "punch," as in a fruity drink, and *zu* means "vinegar" in Japanese. This suggests that the sauce could date back to between the 17th and 18th centuries, when Holland was the only western country engaged in trade with Japan.

Lemon juice	2/3 cup	150 mL
Lime juice	1/3 cup	75 mL
Rice vinegar	1/4 cup	60 mL
Soy sauce	1 cup	250 mL
Mirin	1/4 cup	60 mL
Kombu (kelp) strip (3 inch, 7.5 cm, long)	1	1
Bonito flakes	1/2 cup	125 mL

Combine all 7 ingredients in a small saucepan on medium heat and bring to a simmer. Cook for about 5 minutes, stirring occasionally. Remove from heat and set aside to cool. Transfer to a medium bowl and let stand, covered, in refrigerator for at least 4 hours and up to overnight. Strain mixture through a fine-mesh sieve or a sieve lined with cheesecloth, discarding solids. Store in a jar or airtight container in refrigerator for up to 2 weeks. Makes about 2 1/2 cups (625 mL).

Bonito flakes, also called *katsuobushi*, are dried, fermented fish flakes, either bonito or skipjack tuna, that are used to give food a smoky, slightly fishy flavour. They are available at most grocery stores.

Soy Sauce: A Retrospective

Although soy sauce has a global reach today, it can trace its roots back to ancient China. Early sauces in China were more of a paste than a liquid and were collectively called *chiang* (also written as *jiang*). Early *chiang* were made of fermented meat, but soy-based *chiang* appeared during the Han period (beginning around 206 BCE). This also coincides with the time that Buddhism was introduced to China, and soy *chiang* were most likely created as a meat-free alternative for Buddhists, who do not believe in harming animals. Soy *chiang* was the predominate seasoning in China until the 17th century, when people began to choose liquid sauces over pastes, and soy sauce began to overtake soy *chiang* in popularity.

Thanks to historical trade routes (and past Chinese Empire expansion), soy sauce spread throughout much of East and Southeast Asia, including Thailand, Vietnam, Korea, Japan, the Philippines and Indonesia. As different regions perfected the manufacturing process, they added their own touches to the sauce. Now there are many kinds of soy sauce, and they all vary in taste and texture.

Japanese soy sauce, both *tamari* and *shoyu*, are most likely local adaptations of the Chinese soy *chiang*. Although there is no clear record of when soy sauce was introduced to Japan, it may have arrived with Buddhist monks around the 6th century. *Shoyu* is made in a similar fashion to Chinese soy sauce, but whereas Chinese soy sauce is made primarily from fermented soybeans, sometimes with a little wheat added, *shoyu* is made with an equal amount of soybeans and wheat, giving it a slightly sweeter flavour. *Tamari* is the byproduct of miso production, and because it has a higher soybean content, it is slightly thicker and has a stronger flavour than *shoyu*.

The history of soy sauce in Korea is not as clear. Although historical records suggest that soybean paste and soy sauce reached Korea in the late 7th century, some scholars suggest that Koreans were the first to experiment with fermentation more than 2000 years ago and introduced fermented soy products to China. Today there are two main types of Korean soy sauce: one type, called *whe-ganjang*, is an all-purpose sauce similar to the Chinese version and was adopted from Japan in the 1880s. The other, called *guk-ganjang* or *joseon ganjang*, named for Korea's Joseon Dynasty (1392–1897 CE), is the traditional Korean soy sauce and is a saltier version used for making soup.

Indonesia is known for their particular style of soy sauce, called *kecap manis*. Although it is often used alongside traditional soy sauce in Indonesian cuisine, it is the *kecap manis* that defines many Indonesian dishes. *Kecap manis* is a thick syrupy soy sauce that seems to have originated in Java in the 19th century. Chinese settlers introduced soy sauce to the area, but the locals preferred sweet sauces, so they added palm sugar to the regular soy sauce, and *kecap manis* was born. The palm sugar gives the sauce caramel or molasses undertones. The sauce can also sometimes contain various herbs or spices, including garlic, galangal, lemongrass and star anise.

So how did soy sauce make it out of Asia to achieve near-global popularity? While we don't have a complete picture of the global dissemination of soy sauce, we do know that Dutch traders introduced soy sauce to Europe from Japan in the 1670s. It became popular in England as a sauce for meat (and eventually as an ingredient in their beloved Worcestershire sauce). British settlers also took it with them to their colonies in North America and Australia. Waves of Chinese migration to Latin America, beginning in the late 1880s, no doubt played a role in introducing soy sauce to Mexico and Peru, and Japanese immigrants have been credited with introducing soy sauce to Brazil in the early 1900s.

Ginger Soy Sauce

Ginger is the rhizome or root of the ginger plant, which is most likely native to Southeast Asia and southern China. Ginger has been used since ancient times, both as an ingredient in food and medicinally to treat digestive issues and other stomach ailments. Its use in China is recorded as early as 500 BCE (though scholars suspect was being used hundreds of years earlier) and the Sanskrit name, *singabera*, suggests it was known in India even earlier (Sanskrit dates back to around 1500 BCE). Although the origins of this sauce are unknown, the combination of ginger and soy sauce is quite common in Chinese cuisine. Use this sauce to flavour rice dishes or as a dipping sauce for fried or boiled dumplings.

Sesame oil	2 tsp.	10 mL
Grated ginger root	1 tbsp.	15 mL
Garlic cloves, minced	3	3
Dark soy sauce	1/2 cup	125 mL
Mirin	1/4 cup	60 mL
Sake	2 tbsp.	30 mL
Brown sugar, packed	1 tbsp.	15 mL

Heat sesame oil in a small saucepan on medium. Add ginger and garlic, and cook until fragrant, about 2 minutes.

Stir in next 4 ingredients and bring to a boil. Reduce to a simmer and cook, stirring occasionally, for 6 to 7 minutes until slightly thickened. Remove from heat and set aside to cool. Store in an airtight container in refrigerator for up to 2 weeks. Makes about 1 cup (250 mL).

Sweet and Sour

The classic pairing of sweet and sour can be found in the cooking traditions of many nations, including Italy, France and England, dating back to the Middle Ages. The Sweet and Sour Sauce we most often think of might be loosely based on a Cantonese dish that paired a similar sauce with pork. This version may have been created in the late 19th century by Chinese workers in North America who adapted their recipes to use local ingredients and to satisfy the Western palate.

Pineapple juice	1 cup	250 mL
Brown sugar, packed	1/2 cup	125 mL
Apple cider vinegar	1/3 cup	75 mL
Soy sauce	1 tbsp.	15 mL
Minced ginger root	1/2 tsp.	2 mL
Garlic clove, minced	1	1
Ground cayenne pepper (optional)	1/8 tsp.	0.5 mL
Cornstarch	2 tbsp.	30 mL
Water	2 tbsp.	30 mL

Combine first 7 ingredients in a small saucepan on medium heat, stirring until sugar is dissolved. Bring to a simmer, stirring occasionally.

Combine cornstarch and water in a small cup or bowl, stirring until smooth. Add mixture to sauce, stirring constantly until sauce starts to thicken. Remove from heat and set aside to cool. Store in a jar or airtight container in refrigerator for up to 7 days or freeze for up to 6 months. Makes 1 1/2 cups (375 mL).

Apple cider vinegar is made from fermented juice that has been extracted from crushed apples. It adds a tangy, bright flavour to a variety of dishes, from soups and stews to salad dressings, marinades and stir fries. Cider vinegar and apple cider vinegar are the same product. The terms can be used interchangeably.

Gochujang

The main ingredient of Gochujang Sauce is gojujang paste, a spicy mixture of red chilies, fermented soy sauce, rice flour and salt. The origins of this paste are unclear, but its use in Korea has been documented as far back as the 17th century, when it was used medicinally for digestive issues. Traditionally this paste was made in an earthenware pot and left outside to ferment for several years, resulting in a paste that was rich in probiotics. The paste is widely used in Korean cuisine and is an essential part of Gochujang Sauce, which dresses the famed dish Bibimbap (meaning "mixed rice bowl") that has gained near-global popularity.

Gochujang paste	2 tbsp.	30 mL
Rice wine vinegar	2 tbsp.	30 mL
Green onions, sliced	2	2
Garlic cloves, minced	2	2
Soy sauce	1 tbsp.	15 mL
Brown sugar, packed	2 tsp.	10 mL
Grated ginger root	2 tsp.	10 mL
Sesame seeds, toasted (see Tip, page 128)	2 tsp.	10 mL
Sesame oil	1 tsp.	5 mL

Whisk all 9 ingredients together in a bowl until smooth. Store in a jar or airtight container in refrigerator for up to 7 days. Makes about 1/2 cup (125 mL).

Cuisine of the Americas: A Historical Perspective

Today we have only a limited understanding of the cultures and cuisines of the Indigenous Peoples who inhabited the Americas before European contact. Most of the information we do have comes either from the archaeological record or from modern-day interpretations of information these cultures left behind.

The civilizations of Mesoamerica had their own unique ways of recording information. The Mayas had Maya hieroglyphic script. The Aztecs used pictograms and ideograms. The Inca used *khipu*, a system of colourful cords and knots that they used to record numbers, though some scholars speculate that *khipu* also included phonetic symbolism and was used to record history, myths, songs and other aspects of Incan culture. These historical recording systems have been studied and interpreted by scholars and archaeologists long after the systems fell out of use, meaning that any understanding we have has been pieced together by people without first-hand knowledge of the systems. This leaves a lot of room for error and misinterpretation.

We have even less knowledge of the cultures of North America pre-European contact because these cultures recorded their history orally, with stories and parables, instead of with written words.

Written records exist for some of the Indigenous Peoples of the Americas after European contact, but the accounts were written by European explorers and colonists, and the information is presented through a European lens or worldview. However, the archeological record combined with written accounts has painted a picture of what the cuisines of the original peoples of the Americas looked like.

The three dominant cultures in Mesoamerica pre-European contact were the Maya, the Inca and the Aztecs. These peoples ate a mostly plant-based diet of fruit, vegetables, grains and beans. Maize was a staple and was soaked in lime water, then ground and made into a dough from which they made tortillas and tamales. They also ate potatoes, sweet potatoes, beans, tomatoes, chili peppers and many types of squash. For meat, they ate mostly small animals, including turkeys, ducks, guinea pigs, frogs, fish and iguanas, though they occasionally hunted bigger game including deer and peccaries. The Inca also raised llamas and alpacas for food and hunted vicunas and guanaco. Insects played a huge role in the cuisine of all three cultures, as did the cacao bean, which was ground into a hot drink and flavoured with ground chili peppers and sometimes honey. The Aztecs harvested spirulina, an excellent source of protein and minerals—from the lakes. They are also credited with making two sauces that we still eat today: one from pounded tomatoes, chili peppers and herbs, an early form of salsa, and the other, called *ahuaca-mulli*, of mashed avocado, onion and tomatoes, the ancestor of guacamole.

The Indigenous Peoples of what is today Canada and the U.S. were primarily hunters and gatherers, living off the land. They hunted wild game, fish and waterfowl, and harvested an extensive array of plants, including many types of berries. Some cultures, like the Haudenosaunee, were agriculturalists and grew the "Three Sisters," maize, squash and beans. The crops were planted together so that the corn stalks provided a structure for the vines of the beans to grow, and the squash's spiny leaves provided cover to prevent the growth of weeds and kept browsing animals away.

There is not enough space here to go into the varied cuisines of the Americas since European contact, but it is enough to say that Europeans brought many changes to the lands they colonized, both for the peoples' cultures and their cuisine.

Mole Poblano Sauce

The word *mole* comes from *molli*, a Nahuatl (the language of the Aztecs) word that means "sauce." Often called the national dish of Mexico, Mole Poblano is a bit of a mystery, an interesting mix of Old World ingredients (cinnamon, cloves, black pepper) and New World ingredients (turkey, chilies, pumpkin seeds.) The origin of this dish is contested. Some say it is an Aztec dish and was offered by Montezuma to Spanish explorers in the early 1500s, but this seems unlikely as the Aztecs did not add chocolate to food—they used it only as a ceremonial drink. Another theory suggests that the dish was created in the late 17th century by nuns at a convent in Pueblo, who threw together the dish from the ingredients they had on hand when faced with the unexpected arrival of an archbishop. Whatever the origins of the dish, the rich, complex sauce is time-consuming and labour-intensive when prepared in the traditional manner, so we have created this simplified version you can pull together in a fraction of the time.

Ancho chilies, stemmed, seeded and chopped into 1/2 inch (12 mm) pieces (see Tip, page 160)	2	2
Pasilla chilies, stemmed seeded and chopped into 1/2 inch (12 mm) pieces (see Tip, page 160)	2	2
Vegetable oil	2 tbsp.	30 mL
Chopped onion	3/4 cup	175 mL
Garlic cloves, minced	3	3
Ground cinnamon	1/2 tsp.	2 mL
Ground cumin	1/4 tsp.	1 mL
Salt	1/4 tsp.	1 mL
Pepper	1/4 tsp.	1 mL
Ground cloves	1/8 tsp.	0.5 mL
Semi-sweet chocolate, chopped	1 oz.	28 g
Vegetable broth	2 1/2 cups	625 mL
Can of fire-roasted diced tomatoes (14 oz., 398 mL)	1	1
Raisins	1/4 cup	60 mL
Pumpkin seeds, toasted (see Tip, page 128)	2 tbsp.	30 mL
Chopped dry roasted peanuts, unsalted	2 tbsp.	30 mL
Chopped almonds	2 tbsp.	30 mL
Sesame seeds, toasted (see Tip, page 128)	1 tbsp.	15 mL

Salt, to taste
Pepper, to taste

Toast ancho and pasilla chilies in a medium frying pan on medium-high heat, stirring frequently, until fragrant, about 3 to 6 minutes. Transfer to a plate.

Heat oil in a medium saucepan on medium. Add onion and cook, stirring often, until softened, about 5 minutes.

Add next 6 ingredients and cook, stirring constantly, until fragrant, about 1 minute. Add chocolate and cook, stirring constantly, until melted.

Stir in next 7 ingredients and toasted chilies and bring to a boil. Reduce heat to a simmer and cook, stirring occasionally, for about 30 minutes until reduced to about 4 cups (1 L). Remove saucepan from heat. Carefully process with an immersion blender or in a blender until smooth, following manufacturer's instructions for processing hot liquids.

Season to taste with salt and pepper. Store in a jar or airtight container in refrigerator for up to 7 days. Makes about 4 cups (1L).

Chimichurri

Because it is vibrant green and herby, Chimichurri is sometimes incorrectly described as Argentina's version of pesto, but that comparison sells this delicious sauce short. The flavour profiles of both sauces are entirely different, and Chimichurri is traditionally slathered on grilled meats or used to top other meat dishes, not pasta. The origins of this sauce are unclear, with some historians suggesting it was created by Indigenous Peoples in the Andes of northern Argentina before European contact, and others claiming that it was the brainchild of an Irish immigrant, Jimmy McCurry, in the 19th century. According to this school of thought, McCurry invented the sauce as a substitute for his beloved Worcestershire sauce, and "Jimmy McCurry's sauce" became "chimichurri sauce" when mispronounced by the local peoples.

Lemon juice	3/4 cup	175 mL
Olive oil	1 cup	250 mL
Flat leaf parsley, chopped	1 1/4 cups	375 mL
Fresh oregano, chopped	1/4 cup	60 mL
Onion, finely chopped	1/4 cup	60 mL
Garlic cloves, minced	6	6
Red pepper flakes	2 tsp.	10 mL
Salt	1 tsp.	5 mL
Pepper	1/2 tsp.	2 mL

Combine all 9 ingredients in a medium bowl, stirring until well combined. If not using right away, store Chimichurri in refrigerator, covered, for up to 4 hours. Allow to come to room temperature before serving. Makes about 2 cups (500 mL).

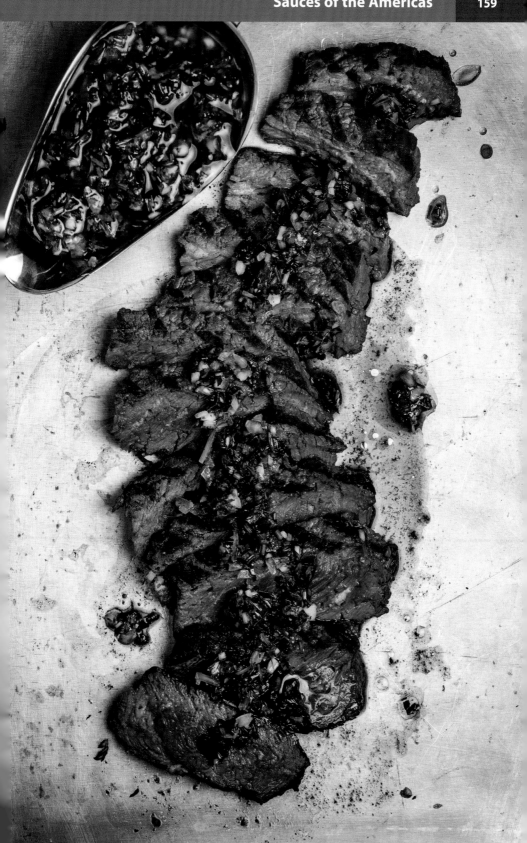

Aji Verde

Popular throughout much of South America, Aji Verde seems to have originated in Peru and dates back to at least Incan times. Although it has *verde* in the name (meaning "green" in Spanish), this sauce in Peru is traditionally yellow, made with aji amarillo peppers, which are a type of yellow hot pepper (*amarillo* meaning "yellow.") Outside of Peru, jalapeños are more often the pepper of choice, but if you can find *aji amarillo* paste in a Latin market or online, add a spoonful to your sauce. You won't regret it. Aji Verde pairs well with pretty much anything from potatoes or rice to tacos or eggs. If you can't find Cotija cheese, use Parmesan instead.

Cilantro leaves	2 cups	500 mL
Mayonnaise	1/2 cup	125 mL
Grated Cotija cheese	1/3 cup	75 mL
Fresh jalapeño peppers, finely chopped (see Tip, page below)	2	2
Garlic cloves, sliced	4	4
Lime juice	2 tbsp.	30 mL
Salt	1/2 tsp.	2 mL

Combine first 5 ingredients in a food processor, processing until smooth and creamy. There will still be texture with cilantro leaves.

Stir in lime juice and salt. Transfer to a medium bowl and let stand at room temperature for about 1 hour before serving. Store in an airtight container in refrigerator for up to 4 days. Makes about 1 1/4 cups (300 mL).

Tip: Hot peppers contain capsaicin in the seeds and ribs. Removing the seeds will reduce the heat. Wear rubber gloves when handling hot peppers and avoid touching your eyes, Wash your hands well afterwards.

Named after the town where it originated, Cotija cheese is a Mexican staple. Made from cow's milk, it has a mild, tangy flavour and does not melt when heated. This cheese comes in two forms: a young version that is comparable in texture to feta and an aged version that is has a texture similar to Parmesan.

Pico de Gallo

Pico de Gallo, also called Salsa Cruda ("raw sauce") or Salsa Mexicana ("Mexican sauce"), is a chunky sauce made of fresh chopped tomatoes, hot peppers, garlic and cilantro. It is an uncooked, drier, chunkier version of the jarred salsa you typically eat with tortilla chips or nachos, and it is used in the same ways. The origin of the name is unclear: *pico de gallo* is Spanish for "rooster's beak," an unlikely name for this tasty sauce.

Roma tomatoes, seeded and diced	12	12
Red onion, diced	1	1
Chopped fresh cilantro	2 cups	500 mL
Fresh jalapeño peppers, finely chopped (see Tip, page 160)	2	2
Lime juice	2 tbsp.	30 mL
Garlic cloves, minced	2	2
Salt	1 tsp.	5 mL

Combine first 3 ingredients in a medium bowl.

Stir in next 4 ingredients and let stand at room temperature for about 1 hour before serving. Store in an airtight container in refrigerator for up to 3 days. Makes 5 cups (1.25 L).

Salsa Verde

The Aztecs are credited with domesticating the tomatillo around 800 BCE, and the word *tomatillo* (meaning "little tomato" in Spanish) comes from the Nahuatl word *tomatl,* the name the Aztecs had for this fruit. Whether or not the Aztecs created Salsa Verde is unknown, but because they are known to have used tomatillos and hot peppers in their dishes, it seems likely that they would have had a sauce at least somewhat reminiscent of the sauce we know today.

Tomatillos, husks and stems removed	6 cups	1.5 L
Olive oil	2 tsp.	10 mL
Chopped onion	1/2 cup	125 mL
Chopped fresh cilantro	1/2 cup	125 mL
Garlic cloves, minced	4	4
Lime juice	1 tbsp.	15 mL
Jalapeño peppers, seeded and chopped (see Tip, page 160)	2	2
Salt	1/2 tsp.	2 mL

Cut tomatillos in half and toss 5 cups (1.25 L) of tomatillos in olive oil. Set remaining tomatillos aside. Place oil-covered tomatillos cut side down on a foil-lined baking sheet. Place under a broiler for about 5 to 7 minutes to lightly blacken skins of tomatillos. Spin pan halfway through cooking time. Remove from oven and let cool completely.

Transfer broiled and fresh tomatillos to a food processor. Add next 6 ingredients. Pulse until slightly chunky, about 11 or 12 pulses. Transfer to a bowl. Cover and let stand at room temperature for about an hour to combine flavours. Store in an airtight container in refrigerator for up to 1 month. Makes about 5 cups (1.25 L).

Jalapeño Sauce

Although the origins of this sauce are unknown, we likely have the Aztecs to thank for the first hot sauces. Spanish explorers in Mesoamerica who recorded their experience among the Aztecs documented the use of chili peppers being mixed with water and added to food, although it is not clear whether the mixture was added to the food as it was cooking or afterwards as a seasoning. This delicious sauce falls into the latter category and is perfect for dunking everything from mozzarella sticks and zucchini to chicken wings or nuggets.

Cooking oil	1/2 tsp.	2 mL
Fresh jalapeño peppers, sliced	10	10
(see Tip, page 160)		
Garlic clove, minced	1	1
Finely diced onion	1/4 cup	60 mL
Salt	1/2 tsp.	2 mL
Water	1 cup	250 mL
White vinegar	1/2 cup	125 mL

Combine oil, jalapeño, garlic, onion and salt in a medium saucepan over medium-high heat. Cook for 3 to 4 minutes.

Add water and cook for 20 minutes, stirring often, until slightly thickened. Remove from heat and allow mixture to cool to room temperature.

Transfer to a food processor and purée until smooth. Add vinegar and blend for 1 minute. Pour mixture into an airtight container and store in refrigerator for up to 1 week. Makes 2 cups (500 mL).

Barbecue Sauce

The style of cooking that we know as barbecue (i.e. cooking food slowly on a grill over indirect heat such as coals) originated in the Caribbean. Spanish explorers in the West Indies saw Indigenous Peoples, called the Taino, cooking meat on platforms built of green wood that were raised over hot coals by sticks. The Spanish called the cooking style *barbacoa*, most likely an adaptation of the Taino name for it, and they took the cooking style with them as they colonized the Americas. As it caught on in what is now the U.S., barbecue styles took on regional variations, both because of the availability of ingredients and the influence of local preferences.

There are now four prominent barbecue styles in the U.S.: Carolina, Memphis, Kansas and Texas. Carolina style is divided into three styles: north, south and west. North uses a vinegar-based barbecue sauce and was influenced by British settlers, who are also credited with adding basting as a necessary step in the cooking process. South uses a mustard-based sauce and was influenced by German settlers in South Carolina. West also uses a mustard-based sauce, but they have also added tomato to the mix.

Memphis sauce is thin and tomato-based, sweetened with molasses and flavoured with a little cayenne or black pepper.

Kansas style grew out of Memphis style and has a thick tomato-based sauce that is a mixture of crushed tomatoes and spices and is sweetened with molasses. It is the most popular sauce style in the U.S.

Texas sauces have a Mexican influence and often include mesquite flavouring or chili sauce.

Cider vinegar	1/4 cup	60 mL
Water	1/2 cup	125 mL
Ketchup	1/2 cup	125 mL
Granulated sugar	3 tbsp.	45 mL
Salt	1 tsp.	5 mL
Chili powder	1 tsp.	5 mL

Combine all 6 ingredients in a small bowl, mixing well. Store in an airtight container in refrigerator for up to 1 month. Makes 1 1/2 cups (375 mL).

Barbecue sauce, much like the U.S. itself, is the result of a coming together of diverse cultural influences. Christopher Columbus brought cattle to the Spanish colony Hispaniola in the 1490s, and Spanish colonists took them to Mexico and eventually into Texas. Pigs, which were the usual meat of choice in the southern colonies because they were less expensive and required less maintenance than cattle, were introduced to North America from Europe in the 1500s by Spanish conquistador and explorer Hernando de Soto. Molasses and sugar came from the Caribbean, and tomatoes and chili peppers from Central and South America.

Homemade Ketchup

Ketchup is one of the best-known and most popular condiments in the U.S., but it is not American in origin. In fact, the original ketchups were a far cry from the bright red, sugar-laden version we know and love today. Ketchup originated in China in the form of fermented fish sauce, which was added to food for a boost of umami. Chinese fish sauce spread to Indonesia, where English sailors encountered it and, because it would keep indefinitely, brought it with them to add flavour to their rather bland food when they sailed. The sauce became popular in England, where English chefs tried to recreate the flavours using locally available ingredients. In the 18th century, versions of fermented English ketchup abounded, using a wide variety of ingredients, including mushrooms, ground nuts, anchovies, oysters and mussels. These ketchups were used mostly for meats, in the place of gravy. English settlers brought their ketchups to the colony in America, where tomatoes were added in the early 1900s, making an early version of the ketchup we know today.

Vegetable oil	1 tbsp.	15 mL
Chopped onion	1/2 cup	125 mL
Can of stewed tomatoes (14 oz., 398 mL)	1	1
Garlic cloves, minced	3	3
Paprika	1/4 tsp.	60 mL
Ground cumin	1/4 tsp.	60 mL
Ground cinnamon	1/4 tsp.	60 mL
Red wine vinegar	1/4 cup	60 mL
Brown sugar	2 tbsp.	30 mL
Tomato paste (see Tip, page 82)	2 tsp.	10 mL
Salt, to taste		
Pepper, to taste		

Heat oil in a medium saucepan on medium. Add onion and cook until soft, about 4 minutes. Reduce heat and stir in next 5 ingredients. Bring to a simmer and cook, stirring occasionally, for about 10 minutes.

Whisk in next 3 ingredients and bring to a simmer. Cook, stirring occasionally, for 20 to 25 minutes until ketchup has thickened. Carefully process with an immersion blender or in a blender until smooth, following manufacturer's instructions for processing hot liquids. Strain through a fine-mesh sieve into a medium bowl, pressing mixture with back of a spoon. Discard solids. Set ketchup aside to cool completely before seasoning with salt and pepper. Store in a jar or airtight container in refrigerator for up to 7 days. Makes about 2 cups (500 mL).

☙ Garum and Liquamen

The ancient Greeks and Romans also used fish sauce extensively in their food. In ancient Greece, *garum* was a popular seasoning made of the liquid extracted from a mixture of fish entrails, salt and herbs that was left to ferment for a few months. The Romans adopted the sauce from the Greeks, and *garum* is mentioned in their ancient texts, along with *liquamen*. It is unclear whether *garum* and *liquamen* were separate fish sauces or simply two different names for the same sauce. Some suggest that *liquamen* may be a Romanized term for *garum*; others posit that *garum* was a higher quality sauce reserved for the wealthy and *liquamen* was a sauce used by the masses. Historical details are pretty much non-existent, so no one knows for sure. *Garum*, once so widely used it has been called "the ketchup of ancient Rome," declined in popularity after the fall of the Roman Empire and pretty much disappeared from the culinary record. Although it has been likened to ketchup, it would have been closer in flavour and colour to Worcestershire sauce (see page 141), which may have *garum* as its distant ancestor.

Dessert Sauces: A Historical Perspective

There are not nearly as many dessert sauces as there are savoury sauces, most likely because they are a relatively new phenomenon. Whereas savoury sauces date back to antiquity, a sweet dish served as a dessert course at the end of a meal dates back only to around the 18th century and is mostly recognized in Europe and North America.

That is not to say that desserts did not exist before that time. Historical record show that cakes and puddings sweetened with honey existed already in ancient Greece and Rome, though they were quite different from modern versions of the same. At Medieval feasts, they did not separate the main course from dessert, and sweet breads, puddings and cooked fruit dishes were served at the same time as the rest of the meal. Louis XIV,

King of France, was famous for the banquets he held, with lavish cakes, pastries and other sweets piled high on the table. And Carême, famous for his classification of French sauces, was also renowned for the fancy, over-the-top desserts he built of sugar, pastry and marzipan. However, in all these cases, the desserts were for the elite or wealthy, not for your average citizen. Even though sugar had been known in Europe since Medieval times, its high price meant desserts were unattainable for anyone but the upper crust of society.

Sugar cane, which is most likely native to southeast Asia or the East Indies, was cultivated in India in antiquity. Indian sugar was known to the ancient Greeks and Romans, though they used it only medicinally. As early as the 4th century, China was producing sugar with techniques India sugar producers had shared with them. After 510 BCE, when Darius the Great invaded and claimed a swath of northeast India as part of the Persian Empire, the Persians became exporters of sugar, as well. Their sugar industry lasted until they were invaded by the Arabs in the 7th century, at which time the Arabs learned the sugar-producing techniques and began producing sugar in areas throughout their empire.

Western Europe was introduced to sugar in the 11th century thanks to the Crusades, when European crusaders waging their holy war in the Middle East encountered the sweet substance. Crusaders returning to Europe brought sugar back with them, and it quickly became a coveted item. However, because it was in short supply, sugar was extremely expensive and out of reach for most people. It didn't become readily available until the 18th century, when sugar cane plantations in the Caribbean, and later, the discovery that sugar could be extracted from sugar beets, brought the price down. Once sugar became more affordable, sweet treats could grace the plates of the lower classes as well as the rich, and the dessert course was on its way to becoming a mainstay in England. There is no way to know for sure when dessert sauces first made an appearance, but recipes for "pudding sauces" made with butter, sugar and rum or brandy appear in British cookbooks by the 18th century.

Strawberry Coulis

The term "coulis" comes from the French word *couler,* meaning "to flow," and originally referred to the juices that flowed from meat when it was cooking. It is not clear when the meaning changed, but today "coulis" refers to a sauce made of pureed fruit or vegetables. Strawberry Coulis is a sweet, smooth sauce that livens up any number of desserts. Drizzle it over ice cream, rice pudding, shortcake, waffles, crepes, panna cotta, cheesecake...the possibilities are endless!

Strawberries, quartered, then halved if large	3 cups	750 mL
Granulated sugar	1/3 cup	75 mL
Water	1/4 cup	60 mL
Lime juice	1 tbsp.	15 mL
Salt	1/8 tsp.	0.5 mL

In a small pot on medium heat, bring strawberries, sugar and water to a simmer. Cook, stirring occasionally, until sugar is dissolved.

Stir in lime juice and salt. Simmer, stirring occasionally, until strawberries are heated through, about 5 minutes. Remove from heat and set aside to cool. Transfer strawberry mixture to a blender and process for 15 to 17 seconds until smooth. Strain mixture through a fine-mesh sieve or a sieve lined with cheesecloth. Press until all pureed mixture has gone through, leaving seeds behind. Refrigerate, covered, for about an hour until well chilled. Store covered in refrigerator for up to 5 days. Make 1 1/2 cups (375 mL).

℘ Although people have been eating strawberries since antiquity, the berries were mostly foraged in small numbers and were not readily available until the late 1700s, when English gardeners began cultivating them in earnest.

Mango Coulis

Mango Coulis is another great dessert sauce, and it is delicious drizzled over ice cream, panna cotta, sponge cake, cheesecake and key lime pie. You could also stir it into yogurt or add it to a smoothie. This sauce is so versatile, it can even be used on grilled meats, such as chicken or pork.

Chopped mango	2 1/2 cups	625 mL
Granulated sugar	1/3 cup	75 mL
Water	3 tbsp.	45 mL
Lemon juice	2 tbsp.	30 mL
Salt	1/8 tsp.	0.5 mL

In a small pot on medium heat, bring mango, sugar and water to a simmer. Cook, stirring occasionally, until sugar is dissolved.

Stir in lemon juice and salt. Simmer, stirring occasionally, until mango is heated through, about 5 minutes. Remove from heat and set aside to cool. Transfer mixture to a blender and process for 15 to 17 seconds until smooth. Strain through a fine-mesh sieve, pressing mixture with back of spoon until all liquid has gone through leaving pulp behind. Discard pulp. Cover coulis and refrigerate for about an hour until well chilled. Store, covered, in refrigerator for up to 3 days. Makes about 1 1/2 cups (375 mL).

⌀ The mango is native to India, where is was domesticated more than 4000 years ago. It was introduced to Europe by Portuguese sailors in the late 15th or early 16th century.

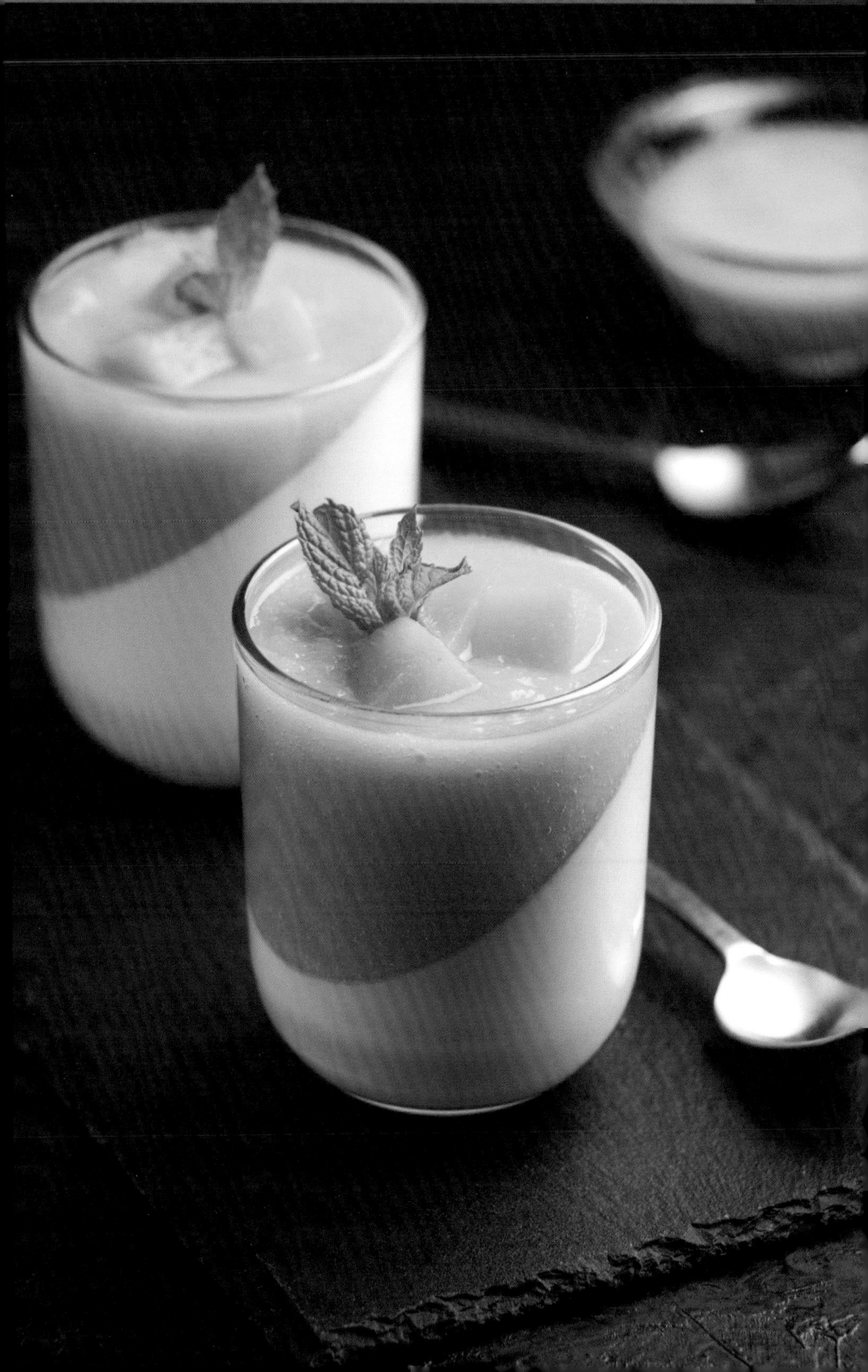

Crème Anglaise

This rich, pourable custard sauce is the most common French dessert sauce. La Varenne included a recipe for Crème d'Angleterre is his famed 1691 cookbook, which may have been a predecessor of Crème Anglaise, though it did not include eggs or sugar. Careme's version, published in his 1828 cookbook, was similar to the sauce we know today, but he apparently did not care for its unpatriotic commonly accepted name and called his sauce Crème Françaises.

Whole milk	1 cup	250 mL
Whipping cream	1 cup	250 mL
Vanilla bean, (4 inches, 10 cm), split	1	1
Egg yolks (large)	6	6
Granulated sugar	1/2 cup	125 mL
Vanilla extract	1/2 tsp.	2 mL
Salt	1/8 tsp.	0.5 mL

Heat first 2 ingredients in a heavy-bottomed medium saucepan on medium. Scrape vanilla bean seeds into milk mixture and whisk until incorporated. Cook, stirring occasionally, until mixture is very hot, and bubbles appear around edge of pot.

Whisk remaining 4 ingredients in a large bowl until thick and pale. Stir 1/4 cup (60 mL) warm milk mixture into egg mixture. Slowly add egg mixture to hot milk mixture in saucepan. Heat on medium-low for about 20 minutes, stirring occasionally, until thickened and mixture coats back of a spoon. Do not overheat or mixture will curdle. Strain sauce through a sieve into a separate large bowl. Serve warm or cover and store in refrigerator for up to 3 days. Makes about 2 cups (500 mL).

ᑫ To make Chocolate Custard Sauce stir 3 oz. (85 g) of melted semi-sweet chocolate squares into Crème Anglaise after it has been strained and while it is still warm (not hot).

Chocolate Sauce

Chocolate arrived in Spain from Mesoamerica in the 1500s and spread throughout the rest of Europe over the next century or so, but it was known only as a drink. It is not clear when chocolate became an ingredient in food, but François Massialot has several recipes in his 1691 cookbook *Le Cuisinier Royal et Bourgeois* that feature chocolate, including one for a chocolate cream sauce. Massialot's cookbook is the second most influential cookbook of 17th century French Cuisine, after La Varenne's iconic book, published in 1651.

Whipping cream	1 cup	250 mL
Butter, unsalted	1 tbsp.	15 mL
Semi-sweet chocolate, (1 oz., 28 g, each), chopped	8	8

Heat whipping cream and butter in a saucepan over medium, whisking constantly until small bubbles start to form.

Reduce heat to low and stir in chocolate. Stir continuously until chocolate has melted and mixture is smooth. Remove from heat and set aside to cool to room temperature. Store in refrigerator for up to 3 days. Makes about 2 cups (500 mL).

White Chocolate Sauce

The history of this sauce is unknown, but it was most likely invented after the mid-1930s as white chocolate was not readily available before then. Who invented white chocolate, and when, is also a bit of a mystery. Made of cocoa butter, milk and sugar, white chocolate may have been created to use up cocoa butter that is left over from the process of making cocoa powder. Nestle is credited with creating the first commercially available white chocolate bar around 1936, but evidence suggests white chocolate was being made in Switzerland at least 20 years before that.

Granulated sugar	1/4 cup	60 mL
Whipping cream	1 cup	250 mL
Vanilla	1 tsp.	5 mL
Brandy (or 1/2 tsp., 2 mL, brandy flavouring)	2 tbsp.	30 mL
White chocolate baking squares (1 oz., 28 g, each), chopped	6	6

Combine sugar and whipping cream in a heavy medium saucepan. Heat, stirring, on medium for 1 to 2 minutes until sugar is dissolved. Boil gently for 3 minutes.

Stir in vanilla and brandy. Remove from heat.

Stir in chocolate until melted and sauce is smooth. Set aside to cool to room temperature. Store in an airtight container in refrigerator for up to 3 days. Makes about 1 2/3 cups (400 mL).

The grayish-white film on chocolate is called bloom and is the result of cocoa butter or sugar crystals rising to the surface after exposure to varying temperatures. It does not affect flavour and after the chocolate is melted, it will disappear.

Chocolate Sauce

Caramel Sauce

The origins of this sauce have been lost to history. Hard caramel candies were being made in the U.S. by at least the mid-17th century, and chewy caramels were known by the 1850s. Whether caramel sauce came before or after caramel candies is anyone's guess. This delicious buttery sauce is great not only over ice cream, but over sticky toffee pudding and even apple pie. It is good served warm as well as room temperature.

Whipping cream	1/2 cup	125 mL
Butter, unsalted	1/2 cup	125 mL
Brown sugar	1/2 cup	125 mL

Combine whipping cream, butter and brown sugar in a large saucepan. Heat on medium, stirring constantly, for 3 to 5 minutes until butter is melted.

Bring to a boil and cook without stirring, for about 5 minutes until slightly thickened. Cool to room temperature. Store in an airtight container in refrigerator for up to 3 days. Makes about 1 cup (250 mL).

Rum Raisin Sauce

Little is known of the origins of this sauce, but it may have its roots in an Italian ice cream, called Malaga. The Italians were the first to soak raisins in alcohol, though initially they used wine, and they added them to vanilla gelato. Once rum became more widely available in Europe in the 17th century, Italians used it instead of wine because rum gave the raisins a stronger flavour. The rum/raisin combination caught on in Europe and made its way into other products, such as baked goods, and apparently, sauces. This sauce can be used to top ice cream, yogurt, pudding and especially bread pudding.

Raisins	3/4 cup	175 mL
Dark rum	1/2 cup	125 mL
Whipping cream	1 1/2 cups	375 mL
Brown sugar	2/3 cup	150 mL

Combine raisins and rum in a medium bowl and set aside to soak for 20 to 30 minutes. Drain rum into a measuring cup and set aside.

Combine whipping cream, raisins and brown sugar in a medium saucepan on medium-high. Bring to a boil, and then reduce heat to low. Cook, stirring frequently, for 6 to 8 minutes until sauce is thick enough to coat back of a spoon and holds a line drawn through it. Remove from heat and stir in reserved rum, adding more if necessary to make 1/4 cup (60 mL). Serve warm or cooled to room temperature. Store in an airtight container in refrigerator for up to 3 days. Makes about 2 1/2 cups (625 mL).

Zabaglione

This is a simple Italian custard-like sauce made with egg yolks, sugar and sweet wine. Marsala is usually the wine of choice, named for a city in Sicily where the wine is made. This sauce is thought to date back to the 16th century when it was served as a beverage. The French adopted Zabaglione in the early 1800s and called it Sabayon. This sauce is often served over fresh fruit, especially berries, but is also wonderful over cake, panettone or fruit-filled crepes. You can also serve it in a bowl like a warm custard, topped with fresh fruit.

Egg yolks (large)	4	4
Berry sugar	1/4 cup	60 mL
Sweet Marsala wine	1/2 cup	125 mL

Fill bottom pot of a double boiler with water, leaving at least 1 inch (2.5 cm) space between water's surface and bottom of top pot. Heat on medium-low until water comes to a simmer. In top pot of a double boiler (see Tip, below), whisk egg yolks and sugar until mixture is pale and foamy. Gradually add marsala wine, whisking constantly. Place top pot over bottom pot of double boiler, whisking mixture constantly until it foams and increases in volume, about 7 to 10 minutes. The mixture should reach a ribbon-like consistency and reach a temperature of 133°F (55°C). Turn off heat and continue to whisk until very rich, fluffy, shiny, and thick ribbon-like consistency. Serve immediately. This sauce does not store or reheat well. Makes about 1 cup (250 mL).

Tip: If you don't have a double boiler, set a large stainless-steel bowl over a pot of simmering water. The bowl should not touch the water in the pot below. Keep an eye on the water in the pot to be sure it does not come to a boil and to top it up should the water evaporate.

INDEX